Praise for *Self Help*

"I'm so grateful for and honored by what Gabby Bernstein has done here. . . . One of my dreams was that a respected leader with both self-help and spiritual bona fides would bring IFS to the public in a safe way that did justice to the power of the model. That dream has come true with this book."

— Richard C. Schwartz, Ph.D., founder of Internal Family Systems therapy

"Gabrielle is the real thing. I respect her work immensely."

— Dr. Wayne Dyer

"A role model for spiritual seekers."

— *The New York Times*

Named "a new thought leader"

by **Oprah's Super Soul Sunday**

SELF HELP

SELF HELP

THIS IS YOUR CHANCE TO CHANGE YOUR LIFE

GABRIELLE BERNSTEIN

HAY HOUSE

HAY HOUSE LLC
Carlsbad, California • New York City
London • Sydney • New Delhi

Published in the United States by:
Hay House LLC: www.hayhouse.com®
Published in Australia by:
Hay House Australia Publishing Pty Ltd: www.hayhouse.com.au
Published in the United Kingdom by:
Hay House UK Ltd: www.hayhouse.co.uk
Published in India by:
Hay House Publishers (India) Pvt Ltd: www.hayhouse.co.in

Cover design: Pete Garceau
Interior design: Julie Davison
Indexer: Beverlee Day

Cataloging-in-Publication Data is on file at the Library of Congress

Hardcover ISBN: 978-1-4019-7666-8
Autographed Edition ISBN: 978-1-4019-9452-5
E-book ISBN: 978-1-4019-7667-5

10 9 8 7 6 5 4 3 2 1
1st edition, December 2024

Printed in the United States of America

This product uses responsibly sourced papers and/or recycled materials. For more information, see www.hayhouse.com.

For Dick, my hero.
Thank you for your friendship,
guidance, and unwavering
faith in this book.

CONTENTS

To enhance your experience,
I have recorded the meditations
and exercises included in the book.
Simply point your smartphone at
the QR code below to find out how
to access these recordings
and other resources.

Xo,
Gabby

(DearGabby.com/SelfHelpResources)

FOREWORD

I just finished reading this book, and there are tears in my eyes. I'm so grateful for and honored by what Gabby Bernstein has done here. I developed Internal Family Systems (IFS) therapy, the approach she features in this book, over the past four decades and labored in relative obscurity for three of those decades. One of my dreams during those lean years was that a respected leader with both self-help and spiritual bona fides would bring IFS to the public in a safe way that did justice to the power of the model. That dream has come true with this book.

I have spent my career training therapists to bring IFS to their clients but always knew that, if translated well, it could become a daily practice that could improve people's lives and relationships. I just didn't know how to do that translation. Enter Gabby. She reached out to me about four years ago to be on her podcast. At that point I had heard her name but would have been much more nervous if I'd known what a big deal she is. We had a great conversation, and I was impressed with how she had done her homework and was so excited about IFS. That led to many subsequent casual conversations—we've become friends—and I was thrilled when she decided to take the level 1 IFS training.

Until I read this book, however, I didn't realize how much she had been using IFS on herself (much of it on her own) and what an impact that work has had on her ability to become what I call Self-led. When she told me she wanted to write a book guiding her audience to use it on themselves, I was excited but also a bit worried. One reason I hadn't pursued bringing this approach directly to the public was because, through years of working with traumatized clients, I had learned how delicate that work can be. This is particularly true once they accessed what I call an exile—a young, vulnerable part of them that was frozen in a trauma scene in the past—a part they had locked away inside. On the other hand, much of Gabby's success has come from her ability to translate spiritual and psychological concepts and practices for the public.

In this book, Gabby has found the solution to my concern. She makes it clear that she is not advocating that readers use the whole IFS model. Instead, she is introducing you to the parts of you that are in manager-protector roles (otherwise known as your ego) and helping you not only get to know them in a different way, but also helping them trust your Self (hence the title of the book *Self Help*), which is a core of qualities like calm, compassion, confidence, and connectedness. In addition, she offers practices and meditations with clear directions to assist you in achieving those goals. If, in the process of using these practices, you do access an exile, she recommends contacting one of the thousands of IFS therapists or practitioners to help you heal that part and then return to your daily five-minute visits with your protectors.

One of Gabby's strengths as a writer and presenter is how courageously disclosive she is, not only of her own traumatic past but also of the extreme roles many of her parts had to take on to protect her. Many readers will identify with her descriptions of her workaholic part, addict part, the controller, the "knives out" aggressive protector, defensive part, self-critical judge, the codependent part, and the perfectionist. Her stories of how these protectors once dominated her life, and now have shifted out of those roles to become inner helpers who trust her Self to lead, are inspiring. As she became more Self-led and embracing of IFS, she was able to stop vilifying each of those inner personalities and instead embrace them with compassion and forgiveness.

There is a lot written these days about how you should show compassion to yourself in a general way, but Gabby's process isn't about conveying care just to the nice parts of you. Through her personal stories, she illustrates the ability to show compassion and love to all parts of you, even the ones that have ruined your life, and to do it in a very specific way that allows them to transform. She calls this her "four-step check-in process," and she helps you apply it to many different and difficult parts of you. You can use this not only in your daily practice of helping your parts but also when someone triggers you. In that case, you learn to do what I call a You-turn in your focus and embrace the protectors that are aroused rather than have them take over and attack the triggering person. Then you can speak for those protectors from Self, which always goes much better.

As Gabby testifies about her own process, the more you make the check-in practice routine, the more your parts come to trust you as a leader, which is one of the big goals of IFS. Then it becomes a virtuous circle: the more they let you lead and see that things go better when they do, the more they trust that it's wise to let you lead. Like "parentified" children in an external family who start to trust that the parents can take over, it's a big relief to your parts to unload all that responsibility, because they are too young to run your life. The more they see you lead, the less extreme and more helpful they become.

With this book, Gabby is paving the way for me and others to find various ways to bring some of the healing power of IFS to larger audiences and make it affordable for everyone.

As I said earlier, this is a dream that's coming true, and I'm so grateful!

— **Richard C. Schwartz, Ph.D.,**
founder of Internal Family Systems therapy

CHAPTER 1

WHO'S INSIDE?

I'm sitting alone in my apartment in New York City with a large cup of coffee next to my laptop. Coffee is my companion when I write a book.

My fingers hover over the keyboard with excitement. While I'm ready to dive in, there's also a part of me that's terrified.

I feel like an imposter. "Who am I to write a self-help book based on the principles of Internal Family Systems Therapy?" The inner voice continues on, "I don't have psychology credentials, and it won't be good enough. I feel stupid and inadequate. I'm a fraud."

Instead of overriding this part of me, I **choose to check in with it**.

Focusing my attention inward, I become **curious**—witnessing the thoughts, feelings, and emotions attached to it. I notice tightness in my stomach and anxiety in my chest. It feels constricting. It's like a knot.

I spend more time gathering information. I know this part of me is female. I wonder about her age. "I'm ten," she says. "I'm in math class and my crush just called me stupid. It feels like a stomach punch. I'm embarrassed, and deep down, I believe him. I suck at math. I can't focus—I'm so stupid."

I'm familiar with this inner critical part of me; after all, she's been around for 35 years. Instead of shutting her down, I witness what needs to be expressed. "I feel so stupid," she repeats.

I notice a part of me that wants to hold her and remind her of how smart she really is. She's a #1 *New York Times* best-selling author in the midst of writing her 10th book! She's gone through training to learn the Internal Family Systems (IFS) Therapy model. She's translated profoundly difficult spiritual and personal growth principles in a way that's easy for everyone to understand. I'm proud of her, and my heart is open now.

I compassionately connect to her by placing my hand on my heart and ask, "What do you need?"

"Believe in me," she responds.

A calm energy of love moves through and my inner dialogue shifts: "Share your own experience—this is your gift. Your stories and lived experience are what will heal."

Sensations of courage emerge. She trusts this courageous feeling—no longer paralyzed by the shameful feelings of inadequacy. She feels hopeful. She feels safe.

I take a deep breath and place my hands on the keyboard.

"Okay, now we're ready to begin."

WHO'S INSIDE?

While this inner dialogue was brief, it would be a mistake to think that it wasn't extremely profound. Even short, compassionate conversations with a part of me that feels inadequate allow me to reset and get back to center.

My ability to stay curious about the fear and remain compassionate toward the inner critic gives me the courage to move forward.

So what was really going on here? How did I swiftly move from fear to courage? How did the presence of compassion seamlessly show up to help? And how did I trust the energy of that presence enough to let the fear step aside?

My ability to care for myself in this way is the result of my commitment to Internal Family Systems (IFS) therapy—the therapeutic model that has changed my life.

As a devoted spiritual student, I've utilized many different styles of healing and paths for spiritual and personal development for over two decades. IFS has been, by far, the most transformative practice in my life. I've seamlessly integrated IFS into every facet of my life—personally and professionally. This includes practicing the model for over seven years with my therapist, participating in facilitator training at the IFS Institute, and introducing the practice to my audiences through my podcast, live talks, and social platforms. This model has affected profound change in my career, my marriage, my parenting, and my human experience. So much so that I've decided to write about and share the miracle of IFS inside this book.

WHAT IS IFS?

When someone says, "Tell me about yourself . . ." what's your immediate response? Maybe you list off your career credentials, or maybe you bust out pictures of your kids to demonstrate your role as a parent. It's highly unlikely that you'd say something like "I'm fun until I get hurt. When I'm hurt, a part of me gets really angry. When I'm angry, I fight back. And when fighting back doesn't work, I shut down and numb out on the Internet."

We identify ourselves based on an outer perception that we've built up over time—what we do, who we parent, our gender, our race, our religion, where we live, etc. Our outer focus and the pretenses we've created about ourselves have masked what matters most: who we truly are on the inside.

Inner reflection is often saved for an hour a week in therapy or a moment on a meditation pillow. Most of the time, our busy lives prevent us from taking the necessary time to reflect on who we truly are, what we genuinely desire, and what we really need. Instead of being receptive to our feelings, we override them. Instead of healing from our difficult life experiences, we shut them down, numb out, and focus our attention outside to avoid what's happening inside. When our external circumstances become challenging and our internal struggles feel overwhelming, we might resort to addictive behaviors such as drugs, alcohol, overeating, gambling, or more. We do this to avoid having to face who's inside.

Facing our innermost feelings and emotions isn't something that comes naturally to most people. Far too often we've been taught to push down, avoid, or minimize our inner experiences. However, within the IFS model, there's a remarkable approach to healing—a compassionate perspective that has the potential to transform your life profoundly. Internal Family Systems is an evidence-based form of psychotherapy that's built on the premise that the mind is naturally made up of multiple parts like subpersonalities. IFS teaches that all our big feelings, thoughts, sensations, behaviors, reactions, and patterns are not *who we are* but are instead *parts of who we are.* We're not one mono person. We're made up of a lot of different parts developed from overwhelming events that took place while we were children.[1]

The goal of IFS is to help you identify and get to know these different parts of yourself so you can relate to your inner thoughts and emotions in a compassionate, kind, and loving way—like an internal family. Through the process of IFS, you can learn to connect to these parts with a calm energy, and ultimately help them feel safe.

THE MAN BEHIND THE METHOD

One afternoon in 2020, I stumbled upon a YouTube interview with the creator of Internal Family Systems (IFS) Therapy, Dr. Richard Schwartz (known as Dick). Within the first minute of hearing Dick explain IFS, I screamed, "That's what I've been doing with my therapist for all these years!" Watching Dick explain IFS so clearly, and recognizing the modality my therapist had been using, felt like the biggest aha moment of my life. I sensed his calm and compassionate energy coming through the computer screen. I was drawn to learn more about this therapy that had been indirectly serving me for so many years—so I bought all of his books and became his student from afar!

Within six months of reading Dick's books, I reached out to his team to invite him on my podcast. I was excited when he accepted but, uncharacteristically, found myself nervous before the taping. However, from the moment he logged on to record, my energy settled.

We had an instant connection. His calm, curious energy allowed me to establish a real feeling of safety within our hour-long conversation. I was in awe of his ability to be so vulnerable and authentic with a stranger. Before we logged off, I shared my plans to take the IFS practitioner training.

"I want to teach this work in some way," I said. Dick instantly agreed that this was the next step for me, and he offered to support me through the process.

IFS was developed in a very intuitively guided way. In his early 30s, Dick was a family therapist with a belief that family therapy was the holy grail. Part of his family therapy practice involved working on an outcome study in an adolescent psychiatric unit treating bulimic patients. He found that his traditional training wasn't getting his patients the results he hoped for. In fact, in some ways it seemed to cause more harm than good. When he'd ask the patient to challenge the bulimia and try to stop the behavior, their self-harm would worsen. Asked why, patients came back with the same response: they expressed the experience of "a different part of them" taking over when they'd binge. This type of response might normally lead a therapist to consider a diagnosis of multiple personality disorder. But instead Dick became curious about the part of them that wanted to binge. His curiosity created a safe environment for patients to feel seen, respected, and heard. As he approached them with curiosity and compassion, the patients began to calm down, open up, and share more about the various "parts" that emerged when they were activated. As a result, Dick made an interesting observation. The extreme behaviors exhibited by these patients seemed as if they were a type of protection mechanism, shielding against deeper, unresolved childhood wounds. Dick began to utilize his family training to help connect with the part of the patient that was struggling with bulimia. He approached the "part" almost as if it was a family therapy session. Except in this case, all of the members were part of the patient's internal family.

For over 40 years, Dick has devoted his life to IFS and helping people recognize the multitude of parts inside them. His therapeutic process has healed countless lives, including mine. "There are no bad parts," he says, offering people a gentle path to recognize all parts of themselves with love and respect.[2]

A GENTLE PATH TO HEALING

IFS is a profoundly compassionate approach to healing. Instead of trying to fix or change yourself, IFS teaches you to become curious and compassionate toward every part of who you are. This can help you develop a deeper understanding of yourself and your inner world, and ultimately lead to greater self-love and acceptance. With a little bit of curiosity, compassion, and courage, you can learn to heal and integrate all the different parts of yourself and create a more fulfilling and joyful life.

A close friend once said to me, "Gabby, I'm having an issue at work. I'm very good at my job and I get along with my coworkers, but the moment I feel challenged by my boss, a completely different side of me comes out. I get super aggressive and fight back. It's like another part of me takes over."

In an effort to know more, I gently asked her, "Is it possible that your aggression is trying to protect you from something?"

I observed her shift her focus inward. Following a brief silence, she replied, "Yes, I've been protecting myself for as long as I can remember."

"Can you focus your attention inside and check in with the part of you that's protecting?" I asked.

She nodded yes.

"What are you experiencing? Do you notice any specific thoughts, sensations, or emotions?" I inquired.

"I'm feeling queasy and nauseous in my stomach, and I'm constantly thinking I need to be perfect and keep it all together."

"How old were you when you first started to protect yourself like this?"

Without hesitation she blurted out, "It started at a young age. My parents challenged everything I did. They tried to make me do things perfectly. I learned that I'd never be perfect in their eyes. So when perfectionism failed, the only way to protect myself was to become really aggressive and fight back. I've been fighting ever since."

This gentle experience of turning inward offered her a new perspective on herself that had a profound impact. All that was required for this shift was her willingness to look inward and become curious, allowing her to witness this experience through the lens of curiosity, and without attack. This moment of witnessing offered her a total shift in perception. Instead of judging her aggressive reaction, she could, in that instance, observe it as a protective mechanism that helped her quell the childhood feelings of inadequacy. This witnessing offered her the chance to see how hard she'd been working to protect herself and the impact it had on her life and her relationships.

PROTECTOR PARTS

We all carry unique defense mechanisms that show up whenever we feel triggered or activated by an external condition, situation, or person. These patterns have been developed over time as an effort to protect against unresolved emotional disturbances from our past—including experiences we may not be consciously aware of. When profound emotional disruptions remain unaddressed, they can become persistent energy patterns in our body and brain. Consequently, we may instinctively resort to fight, flight, or freeze responses whenever an old unresolved emotion is activated. Our unconscious instinct is to avoid experiencing these intense emotions, leading us to take on various behavioral patterns to manage and suppress them.

In Internal Family Systems, what we often think of as automatic reactions, addictions, or habits are called Protector parts. These can be the part of you that resists authority or gives up when things get hard. You might have a perfectionist who works tirelessly to avoid deeper feelings of inadequacy. Or a rageful part, always ready to fight back whenever you feel challenged. Or maybe a people-pleasing part that puts everyone else's needs above your own in an effort to feel lovable. Protector parts are aptly named for their one core mission, which is to protect against impermissible emotions from the past. Feelings that were established at a young age, such as being unlovable, not good enough, unsafe, or even traumatized.

You might notice these parts surface when certain people or situations trigger you. For example, if you have a hard time with authority, you might react defensively when your boss questions you and later regret acting that way. Or perhaps in relationships, you might find yourself getting overly attached quickly, panicking if the other person doesn't respond to your messages right away after just one date. These behaviors can become so ingrained that you may grow to believe that they are *who* you are. But what if they were just a part of you protecting you from some feeling or memory?

Consider this: You are not a control freak, not a rager, not codependent. Instead, you embody various unique personalities, all driven by a common intention—to suppress unresolved feelings of inadequacy, shame, and fear. These parts of yourself have been working to protect and shield you for a long time.

There are two types of Protector parts: Managers and Firefighters. **Managers** often run the show, and these are commonly the parts that are with us on a day-to-day basis. Examples of Managers could be parts that strive for control in an effort to feel safe, or critical parts that judge others to avoid feeling judged. Managers are the Protector parts we rely on regularly to maintain a sense of stability and to block vulnerability or emotional pain.

In situations where life becomes challenging and our Managers' protective techniques no longer work, another form of protection takes charge. This second Protector part is known in IFS as the **Firefighter**. As its name suggests, the Firefighter's purpose is to extinguish the flames of the intense emotions that the Manager can no longer keep down. Firefighters utilize protective efforts that are much more extreme—in many cases they manifest as addicted, harmful, or self-destructive parts.

A Manager and Firefighter dynamic may look like this: A Manager part might show up as highly organized and perfectionistic—the part that insists on creating to-do lists, sticking to a strict schedule, meticulously organizing every detail of daily life, and striving for perfection in work to prevent criticism or failure. This part is around all the time, maintaining its perfectness to avoid feeling overwhelmed, rejected, or judged. However, if this perfectionist Manager part fails or makes a mistake, intense feelings of inadequacy and shame can flood in. When these emotions become overwhelming and the Manager can no longer contain them, a Firefighter part may emerge and engage in more extreme, sometimes harmful behaviors to extinguish the distressing emotions. These behaviors could include self-harm, substance abuse, or disordered eating. Urgent, impulsive actions take over to numb or escape the unbearable feelings.

WHO ARE THE PROTECTORS PROTECTING?

Both types of Protector parts (Firefighters and Managers) are built up to protect against impermissible feelings of shame, fear, terror, and grief that stem from traumatizing and compromising childhood experiences. Let's take a look at how this happens.

As young children (no matter how happy our upbringing), all of us had intolerable experiences, big or small, that led us to freeze and disconnect from life. Our childhood brain lacked the resources to navigate through these intense emotions. Consequently, we suppressed them, shut them out, and buried them deep inside. In effect, we exiled them. But the young, traumatized parts of us that experienced these emotions remain with us. They are known in IFS as the **Exiles**.

All children encounter moments of feeling inadequate or unloved, but when the experience is too intense, bringing deep grief or extreme terror, they do not have the ability to cope with the flood of emotions and process the experiences safely. So the child parts become exiled, or frozen and imprisoned within us, and Protectors step in to suppress the big emotions of the frightened inner child.

Even what may appear to be a minor incident, such as being teased on the playground without a safe adult to assist in processing the experience, can give rise to an exiled part that may remain hidden for years. I've frequently heard people casually minimize their experience when talking about their early years. They'll mention their trauma-free childhood while in the same breath speaking of their parents' divorce or the alcoholic caregiver. These nonchalant references to childhood adversity serve as another means of disconnecting from the reality that something significant indeed occurred and they could not fully process it.

These Exiles carry the burden of inadequacy, shame, terror, or the fear of being unlovable—feelings that were way too overwhelming for a child to handle. And it's these traumatized, shamed, unprocessed emotional children inside us that the Managers and Firefighters work so hard to protect.

LET'S CHECK IN . . .

Okay, so we've covered a lot of ground here, and I want to make sure we're still tracking. Let's recap: we all carry our own unique protection mechanisms, known in IFS as Protector parts.

- **Protector parts:** These are the protection mechanisms within us that respond when we're faced with triggers. They serve as defense mechanisms to shield us from the pain of unresolved emotional disturbances from our past (often childhood).

There are two types of Protectors: Managers and Firefighters.

- **Managers:** These Protector parts are present in our daily lives, striving to prevent our deeper, more vulnerable emotions from reaching our conscious awareness.

- **Firefighters:** When Managers are overwhelmed, Firefighters step in. These Protector parts engage in potentially more extreme, sometimes harmful behaviors to suppress intense emotions related to our past wounds.

The Protectors work tirelessly to anesthetize the Exiles' unresolved emotional distress and trauma.

- **Exiles:** These are the vulnerable parts that carry the weight of our past negative experiences, similar to inner children trapped in a state of distress.

Both Managers and Firefighters work in tandem to keep the Exiles' emotions from surfacing, often through significant measures, to ensure that we don't re-experience the pain of the past.

Does it feel overwhelming to consider that you have different parts inside? Maybe your eyes are glazed over and you're starting to tune out. I get it. It can be a lot for us to contemplate that we have all these little children inside us—let alone acknowledge that there are *traumatized*, exiled child parts that have been locked up for so long. Just bear with me here and suspend your disbelief for a moment. I'm going to gently guide you to open your mind to a new way of perceiving your life. All that's required is your willingness to learn more. The methods in this book won't work without it. So if you're ready for the greatest shift in your life, keep reading and stick around for the miracles. Take a deep breath, put your hand on your heart, and hear me: there are no bad parts of us, and there's help inside.

SELF

What the Protector and Exile parts need—what *we* need—is an internal leader. A leader that can calm the inner children and soothe us when we're flooded with extreme emotions or protective responses. In IFS, true healing comes when we reconnect to our ever-present inner resource known as **Self** (with a capital *S*). IFS understands that an undamaged, wise, resourced, calm, and loving presence of Self exists within us all—and it's available to us at any time.

Dr. Steven Krantz, an IFS therapist, defines *Self* as the "sun behind the clouds." Even though we can't see the sun, we know it's always there. Just like the sun, Self isn't something we have to find, it's already there—we just have to let Self be revealed from behind the clouds of our Protectors. Self is our true nature. If you're comfortable with spiritual lexicon, you might think of Self as your God nature, or Buddha nature, or inner guide. I recognize Self as my ever-present energy of love.

Maybe there have been times in your life when you've felt a sense of creative flow as if you were in total alignment with the Universe. Or maybe you've felt a presence of deep calm during meditation or at the end of a long run. Or you've experienced a sense of expansiveness inside or a fleeting moment of self-compassion. These feelings are the essence of your larger Self.

As children, we turned to our parents to be the Self energy in our life. In many cases, however, our parents weren't capable of meeting our core needs because they—like all of us—hadn't had their own feelings and experiences cared for. So we came to rely on protection mechanisms (Protector parts) to keep down the impermissible emotions that weren't tended to.

Over the years the Protector parts (Managers and Firefighters) grow stronger and stronger and their clouds cover over the presence of Self. Every moment of shame, fear, or trauma causes us to build up an even stronger protective shield. That shield blocks the presence of Self. As we strengthen our connection to Self, we can form an inner sense of safety and reconnect to the supportive resource that we've been longing for.

Self has eight essential qualities, known as the "8 Cs": curiosity, calmness, connectedness, clarity, compassion, creativity, courage, and confidence. These qualities collectively represent an ever-present energy of Self.

IFS teaches that at our core we all have access to these qualities of Self—we don't have to build it up or go get it, it's already inside. When we're connected to Self (even for a moment), we feel as though we're "in the flow"—able to compassionately witness and observe all the feelings and emotions inside. Self is a calm, regulated energy. In that safe state, we have the capacity to notice and witness our sensations, thoughts, emotions, and feelings.

When Self is the leader of the internal family, there's less inner conflict and reactive behavior. When you're connected to Self, your nervous system settles, your inner critics relax, and you feel like you're in the flow.

Even if you struggle to feel connected to Self, you've likely experienced moments of connection throughout your life. Maybe you feel connected to Self for a fleeting moment in Savasana after an hour of yoga, or maybe you feel Self energy come through while you're engaged in a creative project. Self energy can come through naturally when we're creative, engrossed in a physical activity, or in the calm stillness of meditation. While these moments may be brief, they are enough to remind you that Self is already inside. You don't need to repair anything to experience that presence. Simply follow the steps in this book to remove the obstacles to your inherent connection to Self. The more you connect to Self, the more you'll learn to rely on it as an internal guidance system.

Once again, I'm going to ask you to keep an open mind. In the chapters ahead, I will guide you through powerful practices to experience Self firsthand. For now, just remain open. Your readiness and your open heart and mind are all I need to help you unlock the greatest resource of your life.

Take a moment to gently place one hand on your heart and the other hand on your stomach. Take a deep breath in, and on the exhale, release. Breathe in deeply and exhale completely three times. Notice any new sensations in your body. Do you feel a bit more calm? If you even notice the slightest bit of calm or relief, know that it's the energy of Self.

ALIGNING WITH SELF

I had a big-time, hardcore Protector that I called "the workaholic." She authored nine books within the span of 11 years. (Note that while I refer to my parts as feminine, parts can manifest as different genders or be without gender entirely.) She was interviewed by Oprah at age 31—and she built a big business serving people throughout the world before the age of 35. She was praised for her hard work. Even though this workaholic part created a lot of good in the world, she was an addictive part stuck in an extreme role. Her extreme workaholism caused real physical problems for me, including panic attacks, gastrointestinal disorders, insomnia, and ultimately a nervous breakdown.

While I was writing this first section of this book, the workaholic tried to sneak in. I'd taken a few days off to write, and I was solo in my apartment in New York City for what felt like the first time in years. When I sat down to begin the writing process, I started to feel anxious. I ignored the anxiety, poured a cup of coffee, and continued to write. The anxiety came on stronger and my heart started racing. The discomfort was enough for me to step away from my computer to meditate. Turning my attention inward, I checked in with the anxious part. I noticed it and gave it some attention. Within a minute or so, my anxiety spoke up. "I'm making you keep writing. I can't let you take a break because I'm afraid to do nothing. I'm afraid of being unproductive." Boom! There it was: the workaholic part who believed that not being productive meant I wasn't good enough. I was truly amazed that, after all these years, she could just swoop in like that.

Instead of letting the workaholic take over to push past the anxiety, I got curious about her. I put my hand on my heart. I felt a sense of compassion run through my body. My breath relaxed and calmness set in. I connected to my inner sensations of exhaustion. Then I asked that part of me what she needed. "I need a nap," she said.

I listened to the part and gave myself permission to stop working and nap. When I awoke, I felt like I'd had the most profound therapy session. My anxiety was gone, my jaw and face were relaxed, and I enjoyed a nice dinner. Two hours later I returned to my computer to document this story. The writing became effortless. I was no longer pushing; I was flowing. Instead of overriding my exhaustion with the workaholic, I let Self help me.

My commitment to IFS didn't get rid of the workaholic; instead it helped me respect her and care for her. With compassion, I can now thank her for her great work and guide her to do her work in a gentler, softer way. I didn't have to lose my edge; I just softened my edges. Today, this part is still a hard worker, but she's no longer extreme, addicted, and ruining my life. She takes space and cares for her body, and she clears time in her schedule for creative thinking and self-care. She can show up with presence and create even more because she is at ease. And when she gets nervous and tries to take over, she checks in and connects to Self. Oh, and I renamed her. She's no longer the workaholic. She is now "the untethered force of light."

When you're in alignment with Self, your young parts inside feel safe. When a Protector gets activated, you can check in and become curious about what's happening inside, which opens the door for Self energy to come forward. With practice, it becomes second nature to tune in to Self when a part gets triggered. In time, Self energy becomes easier to access in situations that were once controlled by Protectors.

A strong inner connection to Self allows Protectors to feel safe and release their extreme roles. Just like children, parts need to feel seen and soothed. The way to bring the parts back to safety is by connecting to Self energy, which creates a steady presence inside. We will do this in the next chapter with a four-step process I call the Self-help check-in.

This four-step practice is an IFS-informed method that I designed to help gently witness our Protector parts and reconnect them with Self. By establishing this connection, we can create a sanctuary of safety for our parts, allowing Self to emerge as a nurturing inner guide.

Let's take a deep breath and step forward into the next chapter, ready to learn the steps of this gentle but profound process. Here, we will uncover how to bring harmony inside.

CHAPTER 2

THE CHECK-IN PROCESS

My friend Thomas, an IFS therapist, once said, "When I first introduce IFS to my clients, it's like a mind fuck!" In most cases, Thomas is absolutely right. If you aren't spiritually or therapeutically inclined (or even if you are), the idea of turning inward to help out your child parts *is* a jarring concept. So what I'm asking you to do here is no small thing. I'm asking you to transform the way you perceive yourself, which will likely feel uncomfortable at first. That's to be expected. I just told you that you have an inner family of young exiled children stuck in hiding and a whole bunch of Protectors called Managers and Firefighters working their asses off to push down the pain of the Exiles. Then I told you that you have a healing presence of Self energy inside you. Yup, I get that's a lot to grasp, but do your best to stay curious.

In the spirit of curiosity, take a moment to think about one or more parts of you that are managing your life (maybe a perfectionist, or a controlling part, or a fearful part). Give yourself permission to be curious about these aspects of yourself. Open your mind to the concept that they are protective parts of you, shielding deeper feelings. Notice how it feels to focus your attention inward onto these "parts" of you. Is it bringing up uncomfortable feelings? Maybe there's a cynic part of you that's judging these concepts and wants to shut the book. Or maybe there's a part of you that wants to check out and take a nap. When we start to focus our attention inward toward our parts, they can do whatever it takes to deflect the attention. Parts are little children and they really, *really* don't want to face their shame or fear. They get embarrassed and annoyed and they push back. My parts initially hated my IFS therapy because they were too ashamed to be seen by my therapist, let alone by me.

Acknowledging the various internal Protectors and behaviors within us can seem strange and uncomfortable. However, consider the alternative—living in a reality where our Protectors are constantly working overtime to shield us from past pain. When our Protector parts are in charge, our lives can become a cycle of defensiveness, addiction, isolation, and anxiety. It's not an easy way to exist, always on high alert, far from the peace and balance we truly want.

In this chapter, do your best to stay open to this new perception and gently witness whatever's coming up for you right now. While it may not happen overnight, by engaging with the four-step check-in method that I'll present in this chapter—and consistently applying it as you progress through the book—you'll gradually find that the process will become second nature. I've designed this check-in process to act as a guide toward compassionate connection with your parts. I'll be with you every step of the way, and my hope is that you'll stay curious. Your curiosity will offer creative possibilities for profound shifts and a new way of living your life. Stay open to the path I lay out for you.

HOW IT WORKS . . .

The check-in method I present in this book isn't IFS therapy but rather an IFS-informed self-help process. It's my way of introducing you to your Managers (a type of Protector part) and releasing the blocks to the presence of Self (the internal guide). Since we are not in a therapeutic environment, I will not direct you to engage with your Firefighters—the more extreme or addictive protective parts—or your Exiles, which are the vulnerable, younger aspects of yourself, because interacting with these parts can be overwhelming. However, Firefighters and Exiles may come up throughout this journey. If you notice these parts of you arising, gently place your hand on your heart and breathe deeply for as long as you need. If this continues happening, or if you find yourself feeling overwhelmed, I recommend that you work with your parts with a licensed IFS therapist. A directory of IFS therapists can be found at DearGabby.com/SelfHelpResources.

For the purposes of this book, when I talk about a Protector part, you'll know I mean a Manager. By focusing your attention on the Manager parts that are commonly with you throughout the day, you'll get the chance to relate to yourself in a whole new way. My aim is to make this easy and accessible for you to apply on your own terms—anytime, anywhere. I'll do this through a simple four-step process designed to help you shift your perception from seeing yourself as one mono human to witnessing and connecting with the Protector parts who've been managing your life. By witnessing these Managers without judgment, you begin to open the door for the compassionate, calm energy of Self to come forward. I'll guide you to consciously check in with your thoughts, feelings, and emotions and then become curious and listen.

My IFS-informed approach to these steps is different from how IFS is traditionally done in a therapy session—after all, this is *Self*help. Throughout my career as a self-help author, I've been a translator, demystifying spiritual truths and personal development principles in a way that makes them easy for you to understand and practice. In this book I am once again acting as a translator so I can offer you an introduction to the principles of IFS through a Self-guided path. By following the methods inside this book, you'll be able to witness yourself in a whole new way. These gentle methods will offer your Protectors support and help them feel seen. The goal is not to fix them but to witness them with compassion, help them feel calm, and create space for Self energy to come through. When this happens, Self will become your greatest resource and undoubtedly transform your life for the better.

The process of regularly checking in with your Manager parts will empower you and provide you with a new sense of confidence. Instead of spending your days consumed by these protection mechanisms and acting out *as* the part, you'll instead be able to speak *for* the part. Each time you check in using the four-step method, you'll see that the extreme patterns, reactive behavior, and destructive thoughts are not who you are, but instead, a part of who you are. This subtle adjustment in your psyche opens your heart to your parts, allowing you to witness them through the lens of compassion.

NEW NEURAL PATHWAYS AND HABITUAL PATTERNS

By following the four-step check-in and connecting to your inner world, you're creating a safe internal experience, a place where all your parts are welcome, seen, and respected.

Each time you check in with a Protector part, you create a new pattern—a curious connection—that takes the place of your responses to a trigger. The repetition of this behavior will help you establish new neural pathways in your brain. This is why I'll continue to return to the check-in process throughout the book. In each chapter I'll guide you to practice this four-step check-in process to help you create the habit of choosing to connect inward when you're activated—to become curious about the parts that are triggered and offer them support in the moment. These four steps are designed to help you witness your parts through the lens of Self—the presence of love—an intuitive nature that you can trust. This will be the greatest relationship of your life.

My hope is that this process offers you a new way of relating to yourself and an opportunity to feel safe inside. I see this as the ultimate self-help guide that will empower you to know that there is always support available to you—the infinite support of Self. In addition, this book will guide you on your path toward even deeper therapeutic and spiritual development. It may guide you toward an IFS therapist's office, help you on your journey to sobriety, or inspire you to delve deeper into your spiritual practice. This book is designed to offer you an accessible inroad to a new and miraculous way of living.

THE POWER TO CHOOSE A NEW PERCEPTION

There's a famous line often attributed to Victor Frankl: "Between stimulus and response, there is a space. In that space is our power to choose our response. In our response lies our growth and our freedom." This truth embodies the entire essence of the IFS-informed practices in this book. When we slow down enough to turn inward and tend to our Protector parts, we can experience the space "between stimulus and response." In that space, we detach from the stronghold of the Protector, witness it as a part, and clear space for Self to help. This spacious opening allows for Self energy to permeate our being, opening our heart to the activated parts of ourselves, extending compassion and establishing connection.

Accepting Self as your inner guide will help you choose to perceive your parts and your life through the lens of love. The four-step check-in method allows you to create space for making choices. The more frequently you opt for Self-guidance over the fear-driven impulses of your parts, the greater sense of liberation you'll experience within you.

THE CHECK-IN METHOD

Step 1: Choose to check in

By opening this book, you've already made the choice to turn inward for growth and inner development. You've chosen freedom over fear—a choice that's available to us at any moment. Each time you notice you're feeling triggered or activated, that's a signal to choose to turn inward. Instead of overriding your big feelings and emotions, see them as guidance revealing to you that there's a young part inside who needs support. By proactively making the choice to turn inward, you're pausing and pivoting out of the trigger and redirecting your attention inside.

Step 2: Curiosity

After choosing to turn inward, the next step is to become curious.

- Place one hand on your heart and your other hand on your belly to calm your nervous system. Slow down your breath and bring your attention inward.
- Do you notice any feelings, thoughts, or sensations that are inside?
- Where are those feelings in the body?
- What do you know about this part of you? (For instance, does it have an age, image, or story attached to it?)

Curiosity helps you flesh out more information and begin to see the big feelings, thoughts, or sensations as a part of you *rather than who you are.* Curiosity is a form of respect for the part that's coming forward.

As soon as you have a sense of the part inside, it's time to move into compassion.

Step 3: Compassion

Softening more, place your hand on your heart again and take a deep breath. Continue to breathe into the feelings, thoughts, and inner sensations, offering them space and acceptance. Continue this cycle of breathing for as long as you need.

Then ask:

"What do you need?"

This simple question is an act of compassion toward the part. Let the part respond with whatever comes through. Often these parts will say things like: *I need to play, I need to rest, I need to dance.* Be present with what comes forward.

Your parts may respond in ways that are deeply moving to you. By compassionately connecting to the part, you can allow it to speak for what it needs: to feel safe, seen, and supported. And maybe, even for a moment, the part can connect to a compassionate presence inside—the presence of Self.

Step 4: Check for C qualities of Self

The final step is to check for the qualities of Self—the 8 Cs we talked about in Chapter 1. This is a moment to be the witness and feel into your inner landscape.

Check for Cs:

Curiosity: Self is innately curious and willing to explore thoughts, feelings, and emotions from a place of compassion.

Compassion: Self holds the energy of compassion, extending love and kindness to oneself and others.

Calmness: Self is calm and centered even in the most challenging moments. A sense of inner calmness that flows naturally.

Clarity: The Self is your guiding light, offering crystal-clear insights to see situations and emotions with pure objectivity and divine wisdom.

Creativity: Within the Self lies a wellspring of creative brilliance, a sacred source of innovative solutions and profound insights that effortlessly guide you through life's challenges.

Connectedness: Self is the bridge to a profound sense of unity, connecting you with the world and all beings, nurturing a deep feeling of interconnectedness that resonates from your heart.

Courage: Self is your fearless ally, urging you to boldly confront and embrace difficult emotions and challenging situations with unwavering bravery.

Confidence: Self radiates an unwavering self-assurance, igniting the power within you to confidently make decisions and take actions that honor your true values and deepest desires.

When you notice any one of these eight C qualities show up (even for a moment), you can be sure that Self energy is piercing the veil of protection to remind you that you're not alone. When Self enters into your conscious awareness, a message is sent to your brain that you are safe. Each molecule of safety has a profound effect on your emotional state and your nervous system. Compassionate connection helps your parts feel respected for their experiences. The calmness of Self activates deeper breaths and physiological shifts, allowing your body to settle. The clarity that comes from Self allows you to respond and react to situations in a mindful way, clearing space for more creative solutions. As you develop the habit of connecting to your parts, the presence of Self becomes more and more available to you, allowing you to live with more courage and confidence. Spending five minutes a day checking in with a part helps it settle, allowing the C qualities of Self to emerge.

The check-in process will be your guide throughout the book. While each chapter presents unique messages and practices, the check-in process will remain a constant throughout. I've intentionally included the check-in process within each chapter to help you internalize the four steps and eventually integrate them into your daily life. As we progress through the book, I will keep guiding you through the four-step check-in, allowing you to learn more about your parts as the process becomes more natural. In this way, you will gradually uncover a greater sense of peace as you expand your awareness of the energy of Self inside you.

Each chapter builds upon the next, offering you a steady sense of safety throughout your journey. In the next few chapters, I'll help you become familiar with some of your Manager parts (always referring to them as Protectors). Then in the later chapters, when you have a stronger sense of your parts, I'll guide you through practices that will help heighten your awareness of Self. I also recommend that you have a journal or notebook handy when you practice the check-in process.

RESISTANCE TO PARTS

It's perfectly normal if the four-step process initially appears challenging or overwhelming. Often, when people are first introduced to the concept of internal parts, there's a natural resistance or a tendency to disengage. After all, these internal parts have been our companions for years. If you find yourself wrestling with the idea or feeling a bit defensive about it, don't worry—you're not alone. This is a common experience as we start to navigate and understand the complexities within ourselves.

I witnessed this resistance often when I worked as a speaking fellow at a recovery center. I once gave an hour-long talk to the newest group of guests—some only days or weeks sober. As a sober woman since October 2, 2005,

I have great compassion for their suffering and I respect their addiction. In one session, I presented the idea that the addict part of them that has caused so much harm isn't inherently bad. "It's been trying to protect you for a really long time," I explained. "Your addiction was an extreme way of putting out the fire of impermissible feelings of grief from your past."

One man spoke up and said, "I don't believe it's grief makes me an addict. It's my inability to stop drinking." The rest of the audience became restless, with many nodding their heads in agreement.

In an effort to create connection with the group, I shared a hard and personal truth. "It took me a decade of sobriety to even remember the reasons behind my substance use," I said. "At the age of thirty-six, after being ten years sober, I recollected a childhood experience of sexual trauma. The instant I recalled that memory, it became clear to me why I had struggled with cocaine addiction. I had resorted to anything necessary to quell the unbearable and horrifying memory that had been buried in my past."

While this was a scary truth to share, it resonated with the audience. By calmly and courageously sharing my truth, I was able to help them recognize their own.

I then asked the group, "How many of you in this room have faced severe adversity or trauma during your childhood or at some point in your life?" Every person, including myself, raised their hand.

"So if everyone in this room has experienced some form of trauma or extreme adversity, why wouldn't we do whatever it took to numb that pain?" I asked.

The energy in the room shifted again. I could see tears well up in one man's eyes. A room of one hundred people breathed a collective sigh of relief. For a moment they weren't alone in their suffering—they felt seen—and connection set in.

We try so hard to stop our extreme patterns. Stop drinking, stop overeating, stop raging, stop controlling, stop shaming ourselves. But what if these extreme patterns are, in fact, an attempt to protect us by putting out the flames of emotions that are too unbearable to face?

Recognizing the underlying reasons for our Protectors' extreme behaviors can help us access a compassionate perception of them. Our Protector parts are intensely driven to avoid pain, sidestep shame, and suppress past traumas —the Exiled parts. These Exiles embody deep-seated, unresolved emotional disturbances that have shaped our self-perception from a young age. We have spent years, maybe decades, in a relentless struggle to conceal our ingrained feelings of being unworthy of love or inadequate in some way. Our dependence on these Protector parts is profound and pervasive, and without them we'd be left facing impermissible emotions. If we were to lower our defenses, what would remain? We would be confronted with the painful emotions of fear, trauma, and unworthiness—feelings we are desperate to avoid. Therefore, it's understandable that we would resist examining our Protector parts.

The story I was able to share in the recovery center was a tough one to open up about. When I began IFS therapy sessions, I was resistant to the idea that there were younger parts of me inside. For years I'd push back on my therapist, saying things like, "I don't know who's inside me. It's just me!" Over time I began to recognize that I had reactive protective mechanisms, but though I could analyze why they might exist, I remained unaware of what truly lay beneath my extreme behaviors. Then, when I was 36 years old, I had a dream. In the dream I was very young and extremely terrified. I was a small child being sexually abused. In the dream I turned into an adult confronting the abuser. When I woke up, I was filled with terror. At the same time, it was the most palpable feeling of truth—the truth I'd been terrified to face. It felt so real that I immediately shut it down and told myself I'd never speak of it again.

Later that week, during my therapy session, more insights surfaced. My therapist encouraged me to turn my focus inward and connect with the parts of me that had been present in that moment. Suddenly, I jumped off the couch and exclaimed, "It's a child. She's experienced abuse." And there it was. At the age of 36, I connected with the inner child who had suffered abuse. My dream had created the opportunity for my exiled inner child to resurface. The dissociative Protector that had concealed this memory was indeed an extreme Protector.

For over three decades, I built up many Protector parts to keep the exiled, abused child silent. I even named some of these Protector parts. For instance, there was "the controller," who diligently attempted to oversee every minor detail in my life to maintain a sense of safety. Then there was "knives out," the Manager who swiftly responded with aggression whenever I felt threatened. And there was "the addict," a Firefighter part that resorted to drugs to put out the fire of the extreme emotions buried inside. These Protectors were just a few of the many parts within me that tirelessly worked to shield me from confronting the distressing emotions associated with abuse in my childhood. Their job was simple: never let "terrified little Gabby" out.

A less extreme example involves a friend of mine, whom I'll call Sarah to protect her privacy (I'll maintain anonymity in all examples throughout the book). Sarah grew up in a loving household where all her material needs were met. She attended a good public school, enjoyed family vacations, always had a home-cooked meal, and generally speaking had a really nice life. However, when it came to Sarah's big emotions, her parents often dismissed them. They would casually shut her down with comments like "You'll be fine. Just get over it," regardless of what was upsetting her. While these offhand comments may have appeared insignificant, they had a profound impact on Sarah. She never felt truly seen or secure in expressing her emotions, big or small. Whenever her parents said, "You're okay, you'll get over it," it conveyed to Sarah that her feelings were inconsequential, that there was something wrong with her, or that she was too overwhelming. Instead of receiving the emotional support she needed, young Sarah felt ashamed of her feelings. As a result she developed a strong Protector whose role was to shame and blame others whenever she felt upset. Instead of telling people how she felt, Sarah would *show* her feelings with aggression and a negative tone of voice. One of the most potent responses to shame is to "shame back" as a way to deflect the pain.

This Protector has been with Sarah for decades now and has caused a lot of rupture in her adult relationships. She has trouble telling people how she truly feels, and she carries a core belief that her feelings don't matter. Her shaming Protector is always on alert, ready to assign blame or shame the moment she feels inadequate or unlovable.

Recognizing the motivation behind these behaviors may give you pause. You might find a point of connection with either of our stories, or you may feel a sense of compassion for the ways in which Sarah and I have coped with our suffering. Whatever you're noticing right now, acknowledging the motivation behind Protectors is an essential first step toward comprehending the role of Protector parts in general.

The insight gained from this recognition can be transformative, allowing empathy for yourself and others who engage in similar protective patterns. Acknowledging the motivation behind the behavior opens the door for Self-compassion to come through.

By observing the motivation behind the extreme patterns in yourself or others, you can begin to view these patterns as the work of Protectors rather than character flaws. This perspective shift is crucial—it helps you understand that your behavior, habits, and reactions are not indicative of your failure or inadequacy. In fact, they are evidence of your deep-seated commitment to fiercely protecting yourself.

I'm not suggesting that you don't take responsibility for your actions. On the contrary, I believe it's vital to take ownership of your behaviors. However, it's just as critical to address and heal the underlying motivations that drive these behaviors. By doing so, you're not merely treating symptoms; you're nurturing and healing the root causes, which can lead to profound lifelong change.

This empathetic perspective can pave the way for deeper reflection in the coming chapters. Right here, right now, this new perspective has the power to serve as a foundation for the inner work necessary to transform protective parts of you into conscious, healthy, positive attributes.

THE PROMISE

By practicing the four-step check-in process, you can become free from the stronghold of your Protectors and listen and speak for them rather than *as* them. These four steps are rooted in the seat of Self energy. By recognizing in the moment that you have the choice to turn inward, you are no longer the victim of your past. By extending curiosity inward, you're gently clearing space for the part to reveal whatever it needs to reveal. By asking the part what it needs, you're extending compassion and connection. Then by noticing the 8 C qualities, you're reinforcing your own experience of Self energy so that it becomes more apparent in your life. In doing so, you can calmly connect to "the space between stimulus and response." You can tend to the part—and choose again.

When we become curious about the parts of us that are activated, a miraculous shift occurs. The miracle is the shift in the way we feel about ourselves. Instead of judging and attacking ourselves for not thinking or doing things "right," we become curious about the feelings and motivation behind our behavior. Instead of running from, shaming, or numbing our parts, we can befriend them. We can give every part of us the space to be seen and heard, allowing them to feel calm and connected.

Remember, Self is not outside of you, and you don't have to do anything to get to it. Each time you check in, you create an opportunity to reconnect to Self. Each small connection with Self can be as simple as a sigh of relief, a fleeting moment of presence, or a sense of safety in your body. These moments are miracles. When you add up the miraculous moments of Self-connection, you'll remember the courageous strength and wisdom of who you truly are.

Today, my respect for my parts and my connection to Self have changed the way I show up in the world, the way I lead, love, and live. My Protector parts, which once ran my business, have calmed, so my team can safely thrive in a creative space. My defensive part has settled, allowing me to view myself and my husband through the lens of compassion, even in the midst of an argument. Parenting from Self has helped me create a safe, soothing environment for my son. Most importantly, my access to Self has offered me the connection to the parent I myself always longed for. I now know there is a presence of love guiding me and protecting me. Letting Self lead has given me profound freedom and peace.

What will this mean for you? Letting Self lead will allow you to find more success at work. Your relationships will become joyful, safe, and secure. You'll have the confidence to examine addictive and destructive patterns from a gentle, loving, and compassionate place. You'll experience a heightened state of intuition, and creativity, serenity, and safety will be easier to access. I can stand by these promises because I have lived them. The gentle methods in this book will offer your Protectors support and help them feel seen. The goal is not to fix them, but to see them with love, help them feel calm, and create space for Self energy to come through. When this happens, Self will become your greatest resource.

Reconnecting to Self has been a transformational journey for me, shifting my energy, amplifying my purpose, and elevating every facet of my life. My profound connection to Self unleashed my freedom, and it's my divine mission to guide you back to that very same freedom that already resides within you.

CHAPTER 3

CORE BELIEFS

For nearly 20 years, I've been teaching spiritual principles and the power of manifesting. Over those years I've noticed a common trend is that many people tend to overlook the really deep inner work necessary for real and lasting change. The hard truth is that although we can make surface-level adjustments to our actions, true change can only happen when we heal from within and address the core beliefs that block us from manifesting the life we desire. The negative beliefs from our past, our traumas, our suffering, and our pain are all replayed in the present and projected onto the future. Beliefs such as "It's not safe to ask for what I want," "I struggle with money," "I'm not smart," or "I'm not worthy of love" can dominate our consciousness and manifest themselves in our reality. We manifest what we believe.

I get it—most of us want a quick fix or an easy method for manifesting. We want a tool for attracting romance, abundance, or success. The desire for quick change is understandable, and sometimes quick change is even possible. That's because manifesting methods can improve your outlook, your attitude, and your energy, allowing you to attract certain desires into your life. But once you attract what you want, can you keep it? Will you believe you're worthy of it? No. It doesn't last because lasting shifts require genuine, long-lasting change, the kind of change that cracks you open to infinite possibilities and redirects your life. That change requires a deep dive inward.

To create true and lasting change and manifest our desires, we must be willing to courageously confront and heal the repeated thoughts, childhood traumas, and core beliefs that shape the trajectory of our life. I have found IFS to be transformative in this process. When we connect with Self—an inner presence of courage, compassion, clarity, and creativity—we liberate ourselves from the stronghold of our Protector parts, allowing for lasting change to set in. By releasing the burdens of our past, we become free inside and safe to explore and heal the core beliefs that have held us back. When we align with Self and heal our core beliefs, we live with ease, we trust in life, and we can effortlessly manifest.

Reflecting on what I've shared, you may be thinking, "Gabby, how the heck can I change my core beliefs?" I understand it may seem like an insurmountable task, but here's some good news: you're already taking the first steps toward it. Just by being here, reading a book called *Self Help*, you've sent a clear message to the Universe that you're ready and willing for transformation and healing.

Even if your current life circumstances don't align with your deepest desires, trust this: you're already on the right path. Witnessing the parts of you that hold you back from inner peace and a life you desire is the first step toward change. We cannot heal what we cannot see, and we cannot transform what we won't accept. The moments in our lives when we're on our knees, struggling with addiction, going through a divorce, walking away from a career, receiving a diagnosis: those terrifying moments in life are the catalyst for our greatest awakening and transformation. They are the moments that crack us open to the possibility of believing something new. They are the moments when we surrender enough to let Self help.

On the night I sat down to work on this chapter, I received a heart-wrenching text from a friend that read simply: "He asked for a divorce." I immediately called her, and she bravely shared her pain as she spoke about her husband, the man who once fulfilled her greatest desires, now leaving her. Amid her tears, she courageously acknowledged her own role in the relationship, recognizing the need for self-healing. With compassion and clarity, I responded, "This is your opening, sister. When you hit rock bottom, you have the opportunity to heal the core beliefs that block you."

Though my response may not have been the motivational talk she hoped for, it was the truth. Instead of offering quick tips for manifesting a new partner or ways to persuade her husband to come back, I shared the most significant advice I could give her: turn inward and explore the beliefs that hold you back from the love you desire.

Now I offer the same advice to you. This is your moment—the opportunity to heal your past and transform your future. By opening this book, you've set the wheels in motion. With each page you read, you reinforce your commitment to look inward and connect with every part of yourself. This is not only a process of mental reconditioning but also an incredible chance to forge new neural pathways in your brain, facilitating a radical shift in core beliefs—inner shifts that will change your life.

A NEW PERSPECTIVE

Frequently, during my live talks, I ask the audience about the beliefs that block them from attracting their desires. In response I hear the same messages echoing back to me: "I'm not good enough," "I'm unworthy," "I'm unlovable," "I don't have enough," "I don't deserve this," and "I must control everything to succeed." I dig a little deeper, asking how these beliefs make them feel. Common responses include angry, annoyed, frustrated, hopeless, and afraid. These beliefs have amassed such power in these people's subconscious minds that they feel trapped, as if there's no way out of this internal struggle.

During one of my live sessions, a woman in the audience responded to the question with frustration, saying, "I hate this belief. I just want to get over it already!" I locked eyes with her and offered an alternate perspective: "What if I told you that you don't have to get over it, but instead, you can befriend it?" The entire audience collectively sighed, expressing relief at the notion of embracing their beliefs rather than rejecting them. This shift in perspective opened the door to a totally new and empowering approach to dealing with their inner struggles.

As I continued speaking with this audience member from the stage, I gently proposed that these negative beliefs and behaviors were, in fact, protection mechanisms. They represented parts of her psyche working tirelessly to shield her from deeply buried, unresolved feelings from her past that she found too painful or unacceptable to confront directly. In an instant her energy shifted. In a dimly lit auditorium packed with over 1,000 strangers, the energy of the group aligned, and the audience nodded their heads in agreement. This shared connection enabled the audience to borrow the benefits of this one woman's transformation, and the communal energy of Self took hold.

Excited by the momentum of this collective Self energy shift, I proceeded to ask, "When you consider it from that perspective, does it alter how you feel?" She replied, "When I look at my beliefs and my patterns as protection mechanisms from my messed-up past, I feel compassion for myself." In that instant, compassionate awareness opened the door for Self to emerge.

WHAT BELIEFS HOLD YOU BACK?

Take a moment to reflect on any fear-based or limiting beliefs you carry. Is there an incessant inner dialogue you have, like "I'll never be good enough" or "No one will ever love me" or "I have to suffer to succeed"?

Notice one core belief that runs the show in your life.

How does it make you feel?

How does it hold you back in life?

Open your mind even more now. Consider that this belief could be a Protector part trying to manage unwanted disturbances from your past. Consider that this belief is motivated by the defense mechanisms you've built up over time: the Protector parts managing your big emotions and exiled feelings.

As you intellectualize this, you may notice that it makes you uncomfortable to see this belief as a form of protection. Maybe you feel attached to it—so attached that you can't imagine another way of living. Take a deep breath and allow yourself to be present with whatever feelings may arise.

WE CAN BELIEVE WE *ARE* OUR PARTS

IFS teaches that each part inside you carries its own set of beliefs about you. These beliefs often stem from past experiences, conditioning, and emotional disturbances. Each part is like a unique character in your psyche holding tightly to its own set of beliefs. Some parts may hold positive beliefs, recognizing your strengths, whereas others carry more critical beliefs stemming from past traumas. Each part's perception contributes to your core beliefs about yourself, influencing your thoughts, emotions, and behaviors.

I once attempted to introduce this concept to a friend who was grappling with intense self-criticism, believing that he was responsible for anything that went wrong in his world. This was an extremely powerful inner critic—his judgmental part that was so overwhelming for him. Despite this, he was reading my books and was open to my work, indicating a desire to heal and a willingness to try something new. So I suggested we try the check-in process, and he agreed. I guided him to become curious about the critical part within him. "I've been like this for as long as I can remember," he said. He clenched his jaw and fists, as if he were at war with himself. "I deserve to be punished," he uttered through his teeth. It became apparent to me that he "blended" with this Protector part—he fully identified with it. There was no perspective he could take other than this part's. It seemed as if his core beliefs of inner criticism and attack were so ingrained that it was unbearable for him to consider any alternative. At that moment it was clear that his inner critic part was firmly in control.

To help him, I suggested he place his hand on his heart and spend a minute breathing into it. This helped him calm down. I honored him for his courage and acknowledged that we should respect his resistance and come back to this another time. He was so deeply blended with the beliefs of his inner critic that it was important not to challenge it.

In IFS, when someone is "blended" with a part, they believe they *are* the part and are unable to contemplate that there's any other reality. When they are blended, they experience only the emotions of the part. In my friend's example, he lived in a world where he perceived others around him as innocent or forgivable. But when it came to himself, he held himself hostage with self-criticism and attack.

When people become blended with a part, it's common for them to take actions as if they *are* the part. For example, when someone is blended with a rageful part, they might express violent energy or become physically aggressive. In the aftermath of the experience, they may say something like "I don't know what came over me." In their blended state, they acted from the perspective of the enraged part, fully embodying its impulses and emotions, unable to access any connection to Self—as if another personality had indeed taken over. Recognizing when we are blended with such intense emotions may not be possible at the moment—or at all. Some people live constantly in a blended state, whereas others only become blended with a part when triggered. In the case of my friend, he lived blended with his part, unable to see any other reality beyond that perception.

When we are blended, the part can be very resistant to letting down their guard. Attempting to do Self-help in a blended state can really piss off the part that is activated. These parts have worked so hard for so long trying to numb your exiled feelings that they believe it's their only chance for survival. They've never considered another way of being. They're on high alert, always ready to react whenever triggered. Or one may not always live in a blended state but instead fall in and out of an extreme takeover by the part.

A sign that you are blended with a part is when you feel as if "something has come over you." While you may not recognize it until after an extreme outburst or destructive behavior, it's still valuable to witness this blended state after the fact.

At this time you may not be aware of your parts at all, let alone aware of when you might be blended with them. You may still be struggling to contemplate that these beliefs are indeed a form of protection. Even the suggestion of turning your attention inward can be activating. Take your time as you progress through the book, practicing at your own pace and celebrating your openness and curiosity. Honor your current feelings and don't rush. Embrace the healing journey as it feels right for you. If you encounter resistance, allow yourself the space to become curious about it—resistance in itself is a Protector part. Remember, healing begins simply by engaging with this book. Trust your instincts on your personal path to growth, and proceed without pressure. Go at a pace that feels safe for you.

SELF IS OUR INHERENT TRUTH

We all have Self. Will we live in Self all the time? No. But the more we nurture our parts with curiosity and compassionate connection, the easier it will be for Self to emerge. Self is always in the background ready to help—we just need to clear space to receive it.

When we experience a subtle shift in perception—when we choose to witness our destructive, extreme patterns and beliefs as protection mechanisms (Protector parts)—we experience a miraculous adjustment in our psyche. This shift in perception opens the door for spontaneous moments of Self. Fleeting moments of compassion, courage, connectedness, clarity, creativity, and calmness can come through naturally. We can see ourselves differently, recognizing that these parts of us aren't bad; they've just been burdened and stuck in extreme protective roles. Even the slightest shift into Self-perception can be enough to ignite radical inner change.

Self represents our undamaged, resourced, and mature inner parent. It embodies the energy of unconditional love, capable of guiding all the parts within us toward harmony. As I introduced in Chapter 1, Self is the divine essence, the God within us, or the Buddha nature that allows us to navigate our inner world with wisdom and compassion. By connecting with Self, we can cultivate a sense of wholeness and healing, helping us embrace every part of who we are without feeling overwhelmed. Think of Self as our internal parent—the nurturing presence we may never have experienced in our outer lives. Connecting to the compassionate inner essence of Self can dissolve the fear-based, limiting beliefs that have held you back for so long.

Now consider this: imagine having an internal leader that rises up whenever you feel alone, triggered, stuck in addiction, or in need of guidance. This leader is a solution seeker—an energy of courage that speaks up when you can't, a calm presence that remains creative, compassionate, and connected. Take a moment to consider what this would feel like.

Can you feel hope or optimism? Do you feel a sense of possibility? Or do you notice a cynical part that's unwilling to even consider it? Honor whatever feelings are coming through for you. For many people, the concept of Self can be daunting, especially if they have spent their whole lives believing they were alone and uncared for—believing the only way to survive was to remain in their protective role.

Well, the good news is that you don't have to understand Self or intellectualize it. Embracing the consciousness of Self isn't an intellectual exercise; it's an intuitive experience that unfolds within you. So there's no need to overanalyze it—just allow yourself to follow my guidance throughout the book. As you progress, you'll naturally begin to connect with the wisdom and presence of Self, and it will become an integral part of your journey toward healing and transformation. Trust the process, and let your inner knowing guide you on this profound exploration of self-discovery and growth.

PERMISSION TO CHECK IN

Are you feeling open to trying out the check-in process I introduced in the last chapter? Let's see where you're at and make a mindful choice together. Take a moment to focus your attention inward. Ask yourself if there is a particular belief that has been holding you back. Is there a perfectionist? Or a workaholic? Maybe you can identify a part of you as a people pleaser, or an addict, or a controller. Give voice to the thoughts, feelings, or emotions that are most present in your life right now—the part of you that's around most of the time (or all the time). Write it down in your journal, take it in, acknowledge it.

Once you have a sense of a part that is active in your life, I'll guide you to check in and see if you have permission to get to know more about it. You can approach the part with a request for permission to check in and explore it further. You may receive an enthusiastic YES! Or you may sense hesitation or fear, or you may feel entirely disconnected from any part, experiencing a complete blockage instead. Whatever reaction arises within you, honor it completely.

If you feel blocked, or the part isn't ready to check in at this moment, that's perfectly okay and quite common.

No matter where you are, I encourage you to read through the process in the pages ahead and notice how it resonates with you. As I explained in Chapter 2, an effective way to teach is through repetition. The more I reinforce a practice or message, the more likely it is to stick. That's why every chapter in the book will reinforce the four-step check-in process. In each chapter, we'll dive deeper into new ways you can use this process to connect with your parts and tap into Self. The more you practice, the easier it will be to apply.

There's no need to rush; take your time. In fact, if your parts are particularly resistant, it's best to remain curious and learn the method without immediately applying it. We never want to push our parts beyond what they can handle at the moment. Remember, this is a gentle and compassionate process.

If you're aware of a Protector part and feel comfortable checking in with it, then let's take the first step together with the check-in process. Trust your instincts, respect your feelings, and know that I'm here by your side.

LET'S CHECK IN

Step 1: Choose to check in

This step begins with the word *choose*. Choice is the operative word because parts are often young, burdened, and afraid. These young parts likely didn't have a choice in the moments when they became burdened, traumatized, and shamed. Therefore they feel overwhelmed when asked to do something they don't want to do. This process must begin with your buy-in—your conscious choice to turn inward.

Without it, your parts will get more activated and resistant. So always be sure to begin the process by leaning in to the power you have to choose to check in (or not). You may find that you need to read this book all the way through before you feel safe enough to check in. That's totally cool. Just pay attention to how it feels, and never push past the step of choice.

When you feel more comfortable choosing to check inside, you'll be able to use the process on your own, anytime, anywhere. Each time you notice you're feeling triggered or activated, it will be your signal to choose to turn inward. Instead of overriding your big feelings and emotions, see them as guidance—an inner guidance telling you that there's a young part inside who needs support. By proactively making the choice to turn inward, you're pausing and pivoting out of the trigger and redirecting your attention inside. When you choose to check in, you suspend your belief that you *are* the part, seeing instead the big feelings and emotions as a *part* of you.

Take a moment now to see how you feel. Remember, it's your choice to follow this process. What feels right for you right now? Do you choose to check in?

Step 2: Curiosity

Once you make the choice to turn inward, the next step is to become curious about who's inside. Maybe you've named the part, or maybe you've just identified a feeling that you want to check in with. Curiosity helps you flesh out more information and begin to see the big feelings, thoughts, or sensations as a part of you *rather than who you are.* Curiosity is an offering from Self and a form of respect for the part that's coming forward.

I recommend that you close your eyes and turn your attention inward. If closing your eyes feels intimidating, or you find yourself in a place where you can't do so, please feel free to keep your eyes open. Additionally, try not to over-analyze the process. You might have an analytical or cynical part that attempts to understand and intellectualize what you're doing. Notice those parts and gently ask them to take a back seat, making space for the parts that wish to speak up. Trust your intuition; try to simply listen without overthinking the experience. This process is about tuning in to your inner world, so give yourself permission to be present and receptive.

- Place one hand on your heart and your other hand on your belly to calm your nervous system.
- Slow down your breath and bring your attention inward.
- Notice any feelings, thoughts, or sensations that are inside.
- Where are those feelings in the body?
- Do they have a color or a shape? Is there tension or pain?
- Notice what you notice.
- What do you know about this part?
- Does it have an age or gender? How long has it been around?
- Do any images or stories or thoughts come to your mind?
- What else does this part want you to know?

As soon as you have a sense of the part inside, you'll know it's time to connect more closely through step 3.

Step 3: Compassionately connect

Softening more, gently place your hand on your heart and take another deep breath. Continue to breathe into the feelings, thoughts, and inner sensations, offering them space and acceptance.

Take a deep breath and let it out. Now ask the part: "What do you need?"

Listen to what the part says. Try not to question what comes forth, even if it surprises you. Breathe into the response, honor it, and give it space to be seen and heard—fully take in this request. Often these parts (young children) will say things like: *I need to play, I need to rest, I need to dance.* Be present with what comes forward.

Your parts may respond in ways that are deeply moving to you. By compassionately witnessing the part, you can allow it to speak for what it needs: to feel safe, seen, and supported. And maybe, even for a moment, the part can sense a connection to the compassionate Self energy inside.

Note: These protective beliefs have been around for so long that we've grown to rely on them, thereby masking the presence of Self. You don't have to force this process; just gently turn to the part and ask what it needs. This act alone is a profound commitment to the part. Trust that the check-in process has the power to open your heart to the C qualities of Self. You don't have to do anything—just follow the steps and allow.

Step 4: Check for C qualities

Take a moment to notice how you feel. Is your heart more open? Do you feel a bit more calm? Were you able to connect to the part? Look for any of the C qualities of Self: confidence, calmness, creativity, clarity, curiosity, courage, compassion, and connectedness. If you noticed any one of those C qualities (even for a split second), you can know that the presence of Self came through. Self energy is always there, and the check-in process clears space for it to come through naturally.

If you feel called to spend more time with the part, that's great! Keep your eyes closed and just breathe with it. You may feel inspired to pick up a notebook and write with the part. If there's any pull to continue this connection, do not hesitate, just keep checking in. You can do this at your own pace and your own time. It's okay to spend as little or as much time as you wish connecting to the part.

TAKE A MOMENT TO REFLECT . . .

How did it feel to turn inward? Did you shut down and blow off the practice? Did defensive or distracted parts of you show up? Did you yawn or possibly doze off? For instance, early on in practicing IFS I'd notice that any time I'd check in with a vulnerable part, I'd often start to yawn and check out. The instant tiredness was another part stepping in—a dissociative part that was trying to protect against exposing vulnerable parts. All kinds of Protectors will show up during this process to override any feelings of vulnerability or exiled emotions. They are called Protectors, after all.

As you practice this method throughout the book, be conscious of all the parts that come through. You may start the process focusing on one part, only to notice another Protector swoop in to shut down any flood of feelings. Continue to stay curious about each part as it arises. If another part overrides the one you were checking in with, it's okay to shift your focus onto the new Protector that's in the forefront.

If you were able to establish a connection to a part, reflect in your journal on how you felt toward it. Did you feel an open heart or did you feel shut down? Again, there's no right or wrong answer.

How did you feel toward the part?

If you were able to experience an openhearted connection to the part, even for a brief moment, what did that feel like? Maybe you felt expansive, or a tingling sensation in your body, or maybe you felt safe for a second. Did you notice any of the C qualities of Self? Compassion, curiosity, connection, commitment, creativity, clarity, calmness, or confidence?

If you wrote anything down in your journal, take a moment to reflect on it. Give yourself some space to notice the part that came forward; notice any resistance or openness. Give yourself grace with this process. Focusing your attention toward a part can bring up a lot of feelings, or even major resistance. When I started doing this work, I resisted this inner inquiry so much that I'd dissociate, check out, and sometimes even fall asleep. It can take time to establish even the slightest connection to a part of you.

The intention is to help you open up to the idea that you have multiple parts inside, subtly connect to those parts, and notice if there's any Self energy available. Consider this four-step inquiry like riding a bike with training wheels. You don't have to know how to ride a bike; you just hop on and trust that the training wheels will hold you up.

This is a whole new way of experiencing yourself. Like any new habit, it can take a minute to settle in. But once you have it down, it becomes like muscle memory. The repetition of this new behavior will offer you not only spiritual connection but new patterns in your brain. You will be released from the neural loops of fight, flight, and freeze.

You'll establish a new baseline of safety and an inner sense of peace, knowing that there are solutions and that peace awaits inside.

This is big work, my friend. I want to take a moment to honor you for having the courage to look inside. By creating some space to turn inward, you have subtly shifted your perspective about yourself, even if it was for a fleeting moment. When you give parts attention, you open to creative possibilities for connection. The more often you practice these steps, the more encounters you'll have with Self. And here's the coolest thing: Self creates more Self. As you tap into Self energy, it multiplies, because you want more of it. That Self energy has the power to rewrite your core beliefs and put you back into alignment with who you truly are.

THE CARE WE ALWAYS LONGED FOR

Over the years, our parts have shouldered the burdens of our past and assumed roles that have overwhelmed them. They're not bad, they're just burdened by fear. Just like innocent children, they deserve our love, care, and acknowledgment. When we envision these parts as innocent and vulnerable, we see more clearly how much they genuinely need and deserve our attention.

When I reflect on my connection with my six-year-old son, Oliver (my greatest teacher), I can see how each day new parts emerge in him. I understand that I cannot control his life experiences or how his parts react to them, but I can be there for him in the moments when his parts need support—I can create a safe space for him. I offer my curiosity, undivided attention, and unconditional love to his parts. I listen attentively to his inner world, providing a chance for his parts to release the burdens they carry. In doing so, I offer him the guidance of my Self energy as he navigates his own journey of self-discovery and healing.

Unfortunately, the reality is that most of us didn't have parents who were self-help book authors with a dedicated personal growth practice. The majority of people live without any awareness of their own inner parts, let alone understanding those of their children. Most children's education and upbringing don't prioritize—or even include—this kind of awareness about our inner world. However, by embracing the concept of IFS, we have the opportunity to offer ourselves and our children a profound gift—a pathway toward resilience and Self-reliance.

That's where the check-in process comes in. This is your chance to develop your own connection to the internal family of children inside and to your inner parent: Self. The more you strengthen your connection to Self, the easier it is to care for and support the young children inside. These young parts have been burdened and forced into extreme roles and beliefs. They need our daily devotion and commitment to allow space for Self to help. While they may not be as malleable as my six-year-old, they are absolutely capable of reprocessing their past with the support of an openhearted connection to Self. Each time you check in with a part, you offer it the chance to settle down, be seen, and let Self help.

You don't have to take my word for it. Studies show that IFS work can help to heal even deep-seated trauma from the past[1] and that connecting to Self in the present can create a sense of well-being and satisfaction in every area of our lives.[2] There's a growing body of peer-reviewed research aimed at demonstrating IFS's effectiveness in addressing a wide range of issues—from depression,[3] PTSD,[4] and interpersonal conflict[5] to physical conditions such as rheumatoid arthritis[6] and migraine.[7] And every day, researchers are coming to a fuller understanding of the power it has to heal.

Freedom from the burdens of the past does not come overnight. But each time you recognize a part inside and offer it curiosity, compassion, and connection, you offer it the chance to experience a radical shift that affects every part of who you are. Even accepting that it's possible for these parts to experience the Self energy of connection and compassion is enough to change you. Why? Because this process reminds you that the safety you long for is already inside you. So much of our suffering stems from the fact that we were left alone with it. Without a parent or caregiver to support us, we became burdened, overwhelmed, and frozen. When you reconnect with the energy of Self, you'll develop an intuitive presence of calm and safety that you always looked for on the outside.

SELF IS IN EVERY STEP

The check-in process is an IFS-informed self-help tool—a process that will witness your parts and experience glimmers of Self. The C qualities of Self are in each step of the check-in process. I created the process with the perspective that if we lean in to the C qualities such as choice, curiosity, compassion, and connection, we intuitively open the door for Self to set in. Our Protectors don't contemplate the fact that we have the choice to check in, they aren't curious on their own, and it's unlikely that they'd extend a compassionate connection to you. So let the steps do the work. Take all the pressure off. The more you surrender to the process, the more you clear space to be revealed. Self energy will come forward in the most surprising moments. Maybe when you're checking in with a part, or maybe hours later in your journal. You'll begin to feel spontaneous moments of calmness or a burst of creative energy come through you. Pay attention to those moments—they're little gifts from the Universe. Let them add up. That connection has already been ignited, and each glimmer of Self activates a shift inside that will change what you believe about yourself.

All you need is the courage to start the check-in process. Then the Self-led actions inside each step will be your guide back to Self. With the slightest sense of Self, a part can feel calm and more connected. Even a molecule of Self energy can multiply, and the more you check in, the more Self can be revealed.

CHAPTER 4

LET IT OUT

Eight-thirty A.M. is my magic hour. It's when my son is off to school and I'm at my desk and excited to take on the day. I like to write or do creative work at this hour. Unfortunately this creative time can be easily interrupted by one glance at an e-mail or a ping on my phone—I can be sucked into the vortex of my to-dos and lose connection to my creative flow.

On one particular occasion, this distraction really triggered a part of me. As soon as I sat down at my desk, a work e-mail notification popped up on my phone, instantly grabbing my attention and diverting my focus. This particularly troubling e-mail highlighted a mismanaged situation at work that frustrated me. In response, my inner "controller" came forward, unleashing a flurry of responses, determined to regain control over the situation. "I need everyone to step up and get it together!" I repeated, both internally and aloud, freaking out with anger and frustration. Soon after, another part appeared—the judgmental part. I began beating myself up for losing my cool. I thought, "You can't run your business like a ten-year-old." This internal struggle toggled back and forth between two parts—the controlling part and the self-critical judge—leaving me feeling overwhelmed and flooded by the inner conflict.

After a few minutes of obsessing, controlling, and judging, I finally had enough awareness to choose to check in with these parts. I turned my attention inward and noticed my physical sensations: my clenched jaw, the tightness in my face, my stomach in knots. I felt an undercurrent of energy beneath the surface—a combination of rage and sadness. I checked in more by asking the part: "How old are you?"

"I'm young, and I'm freaking out. No one will help me. I have to do it all on my own."

I could sense this part's fear, her sadness, the suffering buried beneath the control. "What would help you feel safe right now?" I asked.

"You can listen," she replied.

This part had a clear message: she wanted space to speak up and be heard. So I opened my journal and let her write freely onto the page. In my experience, when parts write freely, they can feel safe, revealing more about themselves. As I placed my pen to the paper, a gentle inner voice whispered, "It's safe to let it out." With permission to write freely, the part *really* went there—releasing all her worries, rage, anger, frustration, and fear. As she continued to write, I noticed that my body relaxed, my breath softened, and my jaw let go. A sense of calm came over me. In this calm state, the presence of Self came forward as beautiful, compassionate language poured onto the page. Self was there to help.

The controller wrote: *I'm scared to let go. It's so scary to trust anyone.*

Self energy moved through me as I responded: *You're seen and heard now.*

I took a deep breath and received this message, allowing Self to reassure the activated part that she was safe—that she could let go.

TRUST DOESN'T COME EASILY FOR ME

At this point in my personal growth and recovery I know a lot about the exiled parts of me and why my other Protectors work so hard to protect them. The controller carries the burdened belief that she is alone and responsible for figuring everything out. I know why she needs to be in control and why she feels so unsafe letting go. By granting this part the freedom to pause and express her needs, I allowed her to feel acknowledged and understood. I opened the pathway for Self to emerge, reminding me that I'm not alone in this journey.

Writing freely with my parts allows them to let down their guard, clearing space for Self energy to emerge. This journaling practice solidifies my belief that Self is always inside, ready to shine through. This, in turn, allows me to experience more ease at work and guide my company with an emphasis on connection rather than control. As I invite Self in, I cultivate a sense of confidence that I can release my grip and trust that I am safe, even when things at work seem out of control.

Creating space for the Protector to write allowed her to soften. The journal was a contained, safe space to have an emotional tantrum and freely express pent-up emotions. This cathartic release onto the page offered the Protector part relief. I could let out what I was trying so hard to hold in—and I could let it out in a healthy way instead of projecting more rage onto my employees.

My journal has offered me the freedom to let it out and say it all—the shameful shit, the things I'd regret saying out loud, and the exiled fears I could never reveal. Journaling gives me a safe place for parts to come forward and offers me creative ways to honor and respect their needs. When I journal with a Protector part, I can give it space to breathe and settle down. In that calm and clear state, Self energy becomes more available.

In retrospect I recognize that the hundreds of journals I've filled over the years were an attempt to be seen and heard. Little did I know that Self was always there to see every part of me. Inside these journals I can revisit all the different parts that came through. The codependent part, feverishly writing about her fear of being alone, clinging onto her latest boyfriend to feel safe. The achiever part who'd journal for pages about all that she wanted to manifest and accomplish. The cocaine addict part who filled countless pages with terror until she finally came down off the drugs. Piles and piles of journals hold the suffering, the stories, and the extreme fear of my Protectors. I now see how my Protectors relied on those journals for momentary relief from the perpetual noise and burdens they were stuck in.

There is another interesting pattern in my journal entries. Toward the end of every entry, a slight tone of compassion and creativity would set in. Through the fog of inner criticism there was always a glimmer of light. Commonly the language would shift from attack, fear, judgment, and rage to a different voice—a language of love. *Let love in,* I'd write over and over. *Let love in.* Even today, this message never fails to come through onto the page. The message reveals the answer I'm looking for. Because when I *let love in,* I can return to my connection to Self.

Now it's your chance to let it all out to let love in. It's your opportunity to shift the way you see yourself, your patterns, and your past—to see yourself through the lens of love rather than fear. From a spiritual perspective, the perceptual shift from fear to love is a miracle. From an IFS perspective, when a Protector relaxes, Self energy expands. In the absence of our Protector parts, all that's left is love. When we add up these momentary miraculous shifts into Self, our entire life changes. We can establish a deep internal connection to every part of who we are, release our attachment to those parts, and grow an inner awareness of an ever-present love inside. The more these moments of Self add up, the more Self we experience. With calm energy, inner expansion, and an open heart, we can truly cherish every moment of life.

IT CAN BE HARD TO TRUST SELF AT FIRST

While I know in my heart that the loving energy of Self has the power to heal (and I want to shout it from the rooftops), I also want to honor the fact that it can be terrifying to focus attention on what's hidden inside—so scary that we'll do whatever it takes to protect against it. The metaphysical text *A Course in Miracles* says: "It is only the hidden that can terrify, not for what it is, but for its hiddenness." What we hide we cannot heal—we must bring light to the shadows of our past so healing can set in.

We live in a constant state of dysregulation, fear, and unconscious (or conscious) terror of facing what's hidden inside. We've been trained to project our inner feelings outside ourselves, and we look to soothe our inner turmoil with external conditions. Living this way is complicated, chaotic, and extreme, but when we let love in, we can develop trust that there's a gentler, softer way to live.

Being curious about what's hidden inside doesn't come naturally. For example, take a recent encounter I had with a young woman whom I had the privilege of mentoring. We decided to meet at our local coffee shop for a brief catch-up. Almost immediately she began pouring her heart out to me, expressing her ongoing challenges at work. Though she enjoyed her job, she confessed to battling with anxiety whenever she fell short of perfection. "Sometimes I wonder if I should just get another job, or even switch careers entirely," she said in a frustrated tone.

I offered her an honest Gabby kick in the ass, saying, "Sweetheart, remember that *you* go with you wherever you go."

I went on to suggest that the answers she was seeking would come from an inner inquiry, not an outward change. As I was saying this, I noticed her body became tense and she lost eye contact with me. The idea of turning inward was not the answer she was hoping for; I could tell she was disappointed that I didn't offer her a clear, practical piece of advice or a method for manifesting a new job. She wanted a quick fix.

Most people are looking for a quick fix—an outside solution to an internal problem. Looking inside for answers can be confusing and oftentimes scary. Why is it so scary to turn inward? We've lived our entire lives protecting against the beliefs, sensations, feelings, and emotions from our childhood. It was too unbearable to face the pain, so we shut it down. The truth is, though, we actually feel that pain every day. Remember, there are exiled young feelings getting triggered and lots of other Protector parts working tirelessly to keep them hiding. In any moment our exiled (hidden) parts can be activated or triggered—the slightest little thing can set an Exile into activation. Then when the Exile is activated, the Protectors swoop in to lock them back up in hiding. Protectors will do whatever it takes to hide the Exiles' terrifying feelings of inadequacy, trauma, fear, and unsafety. Therefore, even contemplating turning your attention inward can make these child parts of you freak out and often become further entrenched in their extreme role of protection.

When you shine light on the Protectors' fears, they may work harder to keep them in the dark. Protectors don't want to lay down their guard; their job is to manage our feelings and shut down any painful memories, sensations, or thoughts from our past. Protector parts are terrified of being fully seen, so they remain committed to their roles—doing whatever it takes to keep the Exiles hidden.

In truth, being seen is what Protectors need most. These young parts of us need compassion, connection, and a calm presence to support them. But often it can feel terrifying to even give them the slightest bit of attention. Hence, a quick fix or outside solution seems far more appealing than a deep dive inward.

Here's the hard truth: outside solutions to internal suffering will never work. You may choose to end a relationship with an emotionally unavailable boyfriend, hoping to find someone different, only to discover that you attract a similar type of partner in a different physical form. Or like my mentee, you can quit your job because it stresses you out, only to wind up in the same kind of work environment all over again. We cannot make long-lasting changes to our internal experience through outward adjustments. The solutions are inside.

As you take this next step toward getting to know your Protectors, take a moment to ask yourself if you have any fears or concerns about getting to know your parts more.

Do you feel resistant or scared? Are you afraid to turn inward?

Notice what you feel, and don't judge your response. If it feels unsafe to look more closely at your parts, then give yourself permission to sit this exercise out and just follow along by reading the process. All throughout the book, I will reassuringly remind you that you don't *have* to check in with your parts. Just do your best to stay open and Self will take care of the rest. Trust that Self is with you throughout this entire journey and throughout your life. Even while reading this chapter, you may notice some C qualities come through. For instance, maybe you become more curious about the process, or maybe you feel a sense of compassion toward yourself. Take it easy and follow along in the way that feels best for you. If you feel safe to continue this process, let's take the next step toward getting to know your parts a bit more.

SAFELY GET TO KNOW YOUR PROTECTORS

Recognizing that parts may resist this work, I want to share a safe and supportive way to begin connecting through writing freely in a journal. I think back to the countless journal entries I scribed from adolescence to the present. Without even realizing it, I was turning to my journal as a way of releasing extreme thoughts or emotions onto the page—creating a safe space for the parts to calm down. Whenever I'd feel overwhelmed by a relationship, or triggered by a friend, or tempted to take up drugs, I'd turn to my journal to let it all out onto the page. Each entry offered me a sense of calm, anchoring me to myself. After journaling I'd feel a sense of spaciousness in my body and mental relief. In retrospect I can see now how my journaling practice was a bridge back to Self.

When the part can let go freely, a calm sense of Self sets in, offering your entire nervous system a sense of peace. Your mind can calm, and your energy aligns with Self. If you've ever practiced journaling, it's possible that you've felt a sense of relief through the process. Maybe you've noticed that after a long journaling practice you feel more resourced and clear. By letting out what you've been holding within, you clear space for spontaneous resolutions. When you journal, you give the part permission to freely tell the truth. That truth telling allows you to witness the part on the page instead of keeping it stuck inside.

When parts are given a safe space to speak freely, they reveal a lot of what's been burdening them. I liken this to my nighttime conversations with my six-year-old son. Every night before Ollie falls asleep, I cuddle with him in his bed. As soon as he starts to relax and settle, he begins to share a lot of the big feelings and emotions that he's pent up throughout the day. He'll tell me about the boy in class who wasn't nice to him or a grievance he had with me at dinner. These safe, calm moments are his time to let out whatever he's been managing inside. I never try to push past or shut down his big feelings; instead I just hold space and listen, reassuring him that I hear him. Giving him the safe space to speak for his emotions is a profound practice in letting his parts feel seen. In those moments he needs validation and support. It's profound to witness how receptive he is to just speaking his truth in the presence of my Self energy.

Many of us didn't feel safe enough to speak up about our feelings as children. Or when we did, they were shut down by our parents saying things like "You're fine" or "Get over it." Since our childhood emotions and experiences didn't have space to be processed and feel seen, we built up a lot of Protector parts to manage them. As a result of our history, parts have been conditioned not to trust Self. They've developed a way of being in the world in which extreme control seems to be the only safe option. Therefore, allowing them to let down their guard and express themselves may feel overwhelming or even impossible. So be mindful to take it slow and remain curious. Engaging in the practice of journaling with your parts involves creating a space for them to be acknowledged and heard, allowing the release of pent-up emotions. Through this process, your parts find the opportunity to freely express their emotions, accompanied by the support they require when Self emerges.

LET IT OUT TO EXPERIENCE SELF

Whether you've had a journaling practice or not, I'm going to guide you to crack open a journal to hold space for and connect to a Protector part. Through this journaling practice, you'll clear space for the part to safely let out what's been stuck inside. After a period of journaling, you may feel a sense of spaciousness inside or notice some C qualities come forward. Or you may not. Protector parts have been around for a very long time and do whatever it takes to maintain their control of your feelings and emotions, so you may not be able to witness them right away. No matter what the result, the process will have an impact. By offering your parts a safe place to speak up, you're sending an internal message that it *is* safe to speak up.

If journaling is new to you, just think of it as freewriting your responses to the prompts I offer. You can write with no objective or agenda; just let out whatever you've been holding in. When you freely journal without editing, you'll clear space for parts of you to be revealed.

My intention for this practice is for you to let one or more parts safely come forward, speak truth, and release what's been pent up inside. There's a chance you may feel some relief when you're done. That relief is a sign that you've ever so slightly let the part come forward to be seen and have cleared space for Self to come through.

In this journaling practice, I'll guide you first to check in and get curious about the parts that are most present in the moment. Once you establish a bit of a connection, I'll guide you to freewrite for five minutes (or more) to let out what needs to be revealed. If writing with a Protector part feels a bit too weird or overwhelming for you—after all, we're still only in Chapter 4—then consider it a practice of just writing about your feelings. Even if you just think of this practice as devoting some time to journal about your feelings, emotions, or sensations, you'll likely notice relief. Any type of freewriting in a journal helps you let out the voices of the inner critics that have been pent up inside.

Another possible outcome of this practice is that you'll establish a Self-to-part connection. The freewriting practice is designed to help you let go, surrender, and hopefully experience relief. In the absence of resistance, Self is revealed. Therefore, when you let emotions and thoughts out onto the page in a safe, contained way, it's possible that you'll notice Self energy come through naturally. Maybe you feel calmer afterward, or you have more clarity about your feelings. There's no pressure or expectation of the outcome here. Just follow my guidance and see who comes forward. Be present for your parts and let them show you what they need.

JOURNAL WITH YOUR PARTS

Allocate a dedicated and uninterrupted block of 15 minutes for this practice, allowing yourself the flexibility to continue for longer if needed. Begin by taking out your journal and a pen. If you have access to the gabby coaching membership, you can do this journaling exercise within the Self Help section of the app.

The objective of this exercise is to release any pent-up thoughts or emotions. Before we start, take a moment to acknowledge if you have any apprehensions or concerns about journaling with a specific part. This presents an opportunity to express whatever is currently resonating within you. If you do not yet feel ready to write from the perspective of different parts, you can simply journal about the emotions you're feeling right now.

Approach this process as a journey of exploration and strive to stick to the suggested timeline below:

- Set aside 15 minutes.
- Follow my journal prompts for two to five minutes.
- Then freewrite for an additional five to seven minutes or more.
- Leave five minutes at the end for processing.

Find a comfortable seated position at a table, on a sofa, or on the floor. Make sure you're physically settled. I often do this practice sitting on the sofa with a cozy blanket over me. You can follow these prompts in your journal.

To listen to the guided audio of this practice, go to DearGabby.com/SelfHelpResources.

ALL PARTS ARE WELCOME TO JOURNAL

Dick Schwartz often says, "All parts are welcome." This statement is filled with the energy of compassion and inclusion, offering parts the freedom to come forward. In this exercise, informed by a practice Dick created, you'll have the chance to focus your attention on your Manager parts, offering them permission to come forward so you can get to know more about them and gain information and insight into why they've been holding on so tightly to their protective roles.

Have your journal and a pen by your side before you begin the practice.

1. Focus your attention inward and say this statement to yourself or out loud: "I'm not here to change you. I just want to get to know you."
2. Next, say this statement out loud or internally: "If this practice overwhelms me, I will take a break or return to it another time."
3. Next, invite the parts to come forward through your writing: "I welcome any Managers to write with me in the journal and let me know whatever feels safe to reveal."
4. Ask the following question: "What do you want me to know?" Then open your journal and freewrite with your parts. Let all parts come forward as you write and take note of thoughts, emotions, and sensations that you feel, think, or experience.

REFLECT

When you feel complete, take some time to reflect on what came through on the page. Carefully read through what you've written, allowing yourself to gently witness the parts that expressed themselves. Pay attention to any noticeable shifts in your language or a change in the energy behind your words—identify any phrases, words, thoughts, or recurring themes that caught your attention. Underline or highlight these significant aspects that stand out to you.

Here are some questions you may want to reflect on:

- Were there one or more parts present in the writing process?
- What parts came forth? If it feels comfortable to you, take a moment to name the part or parts. Maybe you noticed a judgmental part, or an anxious part. (I like to name my parts because it helps me un-blend from them by seeing them as unique individuals inside me. Seeing them as a part of me rather than *as* me.)
- Did anything surprise you?
- How do you feel toward the part or parts that came forward?
- How did the part or parts feel toward you?
- Check for C qualities. Did you notice words or feelings like compassion, courage, or curiosity, or did you feel a sense of calm, creativity, or confidence? At any point were you surprised by a newfound clarity that was revealed? Did

> you feel a sensation of connection? Take note of what C qualities came through. Even if you didn't notice any C qualities, trust me, the energy of Self has always been inside you.

When I reflect on what I've written in these practices, it usually looks like this: I start with a lot of rage, frustration, sadness—all big emotions, thoughts, and sensations. As I delve deeper on the page, I notice a gradual shift in the tone of my words, transitioning from aggression to a more open and curious mindset. To my surprise, when my questions are driven by curiosity, I often unearth hidden memories, narratives, or even vivid images that were previously repressed. This revelation can be incredibly illuminating.

When I transition into the phase of connection, I occasionally experience a spontaneous sensation of relief while writing. It is as if my heart opens up and I surrender myself onto the pages before me. I can physically sense the relief washing over me, creating a profound expansiveness in my heart. In response I find myself breathing more deeply, and the tension in my face eases, allowing a state of relaxation to set in.

Will this process unfold seamlessly for you right from the start? Most likely it won't, and that's totally normal. You may encounter conflicting Protectors that manifest in your writing with resistance or defensiveness. Initially, it might even be challenging for you to establish a connection and cultivate curiosity. It's important to acknowledge that whatever emerges on the page, the primary objective is to provide space for the part to express itself. If, by the end of the process, what's on the page appears as a long rant of anger, frustration, or any other protective form, that's great too. The goal here is to allow everything to be expressed without restriction. The more you offer each part the freedom to write, the more readily Self will emerge.

WHEN PARTS FEEL SELF ENERGY COME THROUGH

When I take the time to reflect on what I've written, I have a new lens through which I see myself and the Protector part. Instead of judging the Protector, I can see it with compassion. Instead of letting the Protector become more extreme, I've created space for it to be seen and respected, thereby helping the part settle down. When the Protector part settles, I can experience spontaneous moments of Self.

When Protector parts connect to Self, it is like starting a new relationship. You need to get to know each other in order to build trust. Protector parts have a really hard time trusting. They've often felt alone, abused, attacked, ignored, and burdened by the people who were meant to care for them. Therefore, trusting in inner sensations of courage and compassion can feel really hard to do at first. So give yourself grace with this process, and know that by letting your Protector write out all its feelings, emotions, and needs, you're opening the door to let Self in. Release any pressure. Simply being open and willing to engage in this process sends a profound message to all your Protectors that it's safe to seek support. Self is always present within you; it merely requires the freedom to be experienced and expressed.

SELF CAN FEEL FAR FROM REACH

It's very possible that even after this exercise, Self energy feels far from reach. It's possible that when you focus any attention toward a part inside, other Protectors will get activated. It may take a while for Protector parts to let down their guard. These parts of you have been working overtime for most of your life. Sometimes when you ask them how long they've been around, they say, "Forever." Think of Protectors as a habitual pattern of behavior. It's not easy to change a habit or adjust a pattern overnight. The good news is that we're not trying to change our parts, we're trying to help them. Each time you check in with curiosity, you begin to befriend the part, allowing for a deeper connection to Self.

The practice in this chapter isn't easy. I want to acknowledge the courage it takes to give voice to Protector parts. I'm proud of you for even reading through the exercise, let alone practicing it. Your curiosity and willingness to continue reading are a sure sign that Self is guiding you. This 15-minute practice, when applied often, has the power to heighten your awareness of your parts and transform the way you experience yourself. Each time you journal with parts, you send them a message that it's safe. This practice allows you to see the part or parts in their innocence—as a child. This newfound perception of yourself may be fleeting, but the more you connect, the sooner you'll see that the parts are a *part* of you; they're not who you are. An inner shift occurs because you can perceive the part as a protective mechanism rather than labeling it as a "bad personality trait." This clears space for compassion to come through.

It's essential to keep in mind that these parts are young and innocent. By encouraging parts to express themselves, you enable them to unveil their truths and freely express what they need. My son offers me the daily reminder that when you let children speak up, they reveal what *they* truly need. On the morning when I wrote this chapter, I was preparing Ollie for camp, and for 20 minutes I found myself in a negotiation with him about putting on his underwear. He kept resisting and crying out, "I don't want to wear underwear!" Initially I responded with more resistance, assuming it was just typical six-year-old defiance. Eventually I realized that my approach was ineffective, and I chose to offer him curiosity and space to share his feelings. I empathetically asked, "I see this is making you really upset. How can I help you? What do you want me to know about your underwear?" To my surprise, he responded without hesitation, "They're itchy, Mommy." My heart melted. I could see in that moment that I'd spent 20 minutes overriding the real reason for his resistance. He wasn't trying to push my buttons; he was embarrassed to share his needs. Offering him my curious Self energy allowed him to express his needs freely, without resistance.

Parts, like inner children, are simply seeking to be acknowledged and understood. It's our responsibility to connect with the curious energy of Self and actively listen. When you grant a part the freedom to journal openly, you create a space for it to express itself and reveal what it truly needs. Consider this journaling practice a potent tool to get to know your parts and open the door for them to freely communicate their true needs.

Much like young children, too, parts need support rather than resistance. There are no bad children; there are only discouraged children. Instead of shaming or blaming our Manager parts, we can encourage them to voice their concerns, remembering that, as Dick Schwartz would say, "There are no bad parts." When we allow these parts to speak their truth, our hearts have the opportunity to open, and the calm, compassionate presence of Self can emerge.

SIT WITH YOUR PARTS

Take a moment now to sit with the parts that were revealed in this chapter. Review the ideas you reflected on after the journaling practice. Notice one part that came forward, and if you feel called, choose to check in and see how it's doing. This part was courageous and committed enough to come forward, so let's give it some attention and love. Take out your journal one more time for a quick check-in.

At the top of the page, name a part that came forward in the earlier practice.

Take a moment to **choose to check in**.

If you're open to checking in, become **curious**. Ask the part what it wants to share with you now. What feelings, sensations, stories, beliefs want to come forward? How does this part feel right at this moment? Does it like your attention? Or does it not even know you're here? Give it a few minutes to write and share how it feels at this moment. Give it permission to let more out.

Notice if there's any sense of connection. With that **connection, compassionately** turn your focus back to the part and write on the page: *What* do you need and how can I help?

Let the part respond.

Take in what the part has asked for. Now notice how you feel toward the part and **check for C qualities of Self**. Do you notice any calm, curiosity, courage, connection, commitment, clarity, creativity, or compassion? If any C qualities come forward, take a minute or more to breathe into the feeling inside. Allow Self to expand inside you. Let Self in, let love in.

CHAPTER 5

CHOOSE TO CHANGE YOUR LIFE

I step into my usual nail salon. The woman at the register cringes, and the nail techs exchange smirks. I feel embarrassment wash over me. You see, I've become something of a legend at this nail salon, for all the wrong reasons. During nearly every visit, I find myself overwhelmed by an intense sense of panic that seems disproportionate to the simple task of choosing a nail polish color. When I reach the stage of selecting a color, I am overcome by inner turmoil and anxiety that's visible to everyone—and often leads to an impulsive choice that I later regret. This color selection drama has caused me no shortage of stress, embarrassment, and unnecessary expense when I inevitably redo my nails the very next day.

So why is this such a huge issue for me? Isn't having trouble picking out a nail color just about the biggest luxury problem on the planet? It is. But for me it's a major trigger that activates an exiled child part of me. She's a five-year-old crying every morning for her pigtails to be perfect. "No bumps, no bumps!" she screams. She's in the kitchen stamping her feet in outrage, desperately trying to control the one thing she feels she can—the bumps in her pigtails. As I write about her, my heart opens and I feel a deep sense of compassion. I see her clearly and I understand her suffering. She's trying to exercise control in a world where she has none. As I connect with her in this moment, I can feel a deep longing for perfection—for flawless pigtails as a way to maintain control in a world that otherwise feels chaotic.

I spend time with this little girl every two weeks. Blended together, we enter the nail salon with the best of intentions, but always leave disappointed, resentful, and overwhelmed. My husband begs me to stop getting my nails done: "It makes you crazy. Why keep doing this?" I ignore his advice and continue to go back for more.

In reality, each time I step into the nail salon I have a choice—a choice far beyond the color of my nails. I can choose to become flooded by the trigger that activates my wound, totally flip out, embarrass myself, and make a scene. Or I can choose to turn inward, check in, and become curious. But knowing that I have this option and actually choosing it are altogether different challenges.

With all the self-help, therapy, and spiritual tools under my belt, I still eff this up. It's like I go into a comatose state each time I walk into the nail salon. I depart from any semblance of Self-awareness and I fall right back into the trap of feeling flooded and out of control. But instead of beating myself up about these setbacks or pretending they're not a big deal, I choose to perceive these moments as divine assignments for Self-growth and connection. Interestingly, the most seemingly insignificant issues in our lives reveal our deepest wounds. Sweating the small stuff is another form of protection. As long as we're focused on the small stuff, we don't have to focus on the big stuff. Yet if we're willing to allow it, the small stuff can unveil important messages from our Protectors—that's where our power of choice becomes significant.

CHOICE IS A PRACTICE

Can you recall the last time you lost your cool over something seemingly insignificant? Occasionally, when we find ourselves triggered, we can muster enough self-awareness to distance ourselves from the situation, refrain from impulsive texting, pause for a deep breath, or hold our tongue before reacting. But far too often we don't remember we have a choice. We become so consumed by the part that we forget we have the choice to turn inward instead of flipping out. Most of the time, we can live oscillating between parts and their reactive feelings and behaviors. Our Exiles are like a live wire that's hot beneath the surface, while our Protectors work tirelessly to manage the intensity. However, the option to embrace Self is always within our reach, even though it might seem distant at times.

Choice is like a muscle that strengthens with use. It's your anchor when you want to pick up a drink, lash out at your spouse, or binge-eat over your feelings. Choice can redirect you when your Exiles overwhelm you. With each conscious choice, you're building a calm, connected presence within—the presence of Self that transcends the fears of the world.

For decades I've shared spiritual principles through my books, talks, and podcasts. People from all over the world have reached out to me with questions about trauma, addiction, domestic violence, and other challenging issues. When this took place at a live talk, my husband would sit on the edge of his seat, worried that an issue might be too extreme for me to address in such a setting. And yet, with every question, I would deliver the precise message that each person needed to hear.

"How do you do it?" Zach would ask.

"I simply remind them that they have the power to choose again. The answer to any problem can be revealed when we choose to turn inward for guidance."

Looking back, I can see that even before I was consciously aware of Internal Family Systems, I was relying on the concept of choice as a guide back to the Self. This gentle reminder is a testament to the fact that choice serves as the catalyst for our most profound healing. Inside all of us lies an intuitive guide, Self, ready to support us and reveal the next right action.

When you remember that you have the choice to turn inward, you allow Self in. Choosing to turn inward opens your consciousness to the fact that there is a presence of love inside that can genuinely help. Exercising choice reminds you to become the nonjudgmental witness of your Protector parts. Rather than overriding, ignoring, or even shaming your parts, you'll become curious about them, clearing space for important information to be revealed.

Witnessing your Protectors helps them feel seen, respected, and honored. Each time you choose to turn inward to check in with a part, it's like a caring parent coming to support you through your intense emotions. Your choice to turn inward activates the presence of Self, providing hope, safety, and clear direction.

THE CHOICE TO HEAL

Have you ever had an experience of both resentment and relief? Maybe you were at a crossroads between the life you once knew and the path to a new way of living. Perhaps it was a 12-Step meeting or a recovery center where you were torn between frustration and an overwhelming sense of release. Or the day you finally walked out of the house, ending an abusive relationship—finally free, but terrified of what it would mean to be on your own.

Let me take you back to that moment when I walked into a sober recovery room, standing on the precipice of a decision that would redefine the trajectory of my life. I remember the chaos of my addiction to cocaine, alcohol, codependency, and work. Addiction ruled my life. And then, on October 2, 2005, I made a choice to walk into that recovery room and begin my healing journey. Resentment and relief coexisted that day.

That day, I consciously chose to enter a room that held something I couldn't fully grasp, words that seemed foreign but resonated deeply. The group shared a vulnerability and connection I'd never seen before. And although it was unfamiliar, I knew I was home. I had found my people, my community, and most importantly, I'd finally made a choice.

Think back to the day you began your own healing path, whatever that may look like for you. Maybe a friend gave you this book, but the ultimate choice was yours to open it. A choice to wake up, to face your truth, and to embark on the unknown yet hopeful path forward. No matter how extreme your parts may be right now, by opening this book you've made a choice—the choice to let Self help.

As we begin to observe and embrace the fact that we possess the power to heal in any given moment, we unlock an invisible door for Self energy to flow through. If we don't embrace and trust this choice, we remain trapped in the belief that we are merely victims of our triggers and the reactive nature of our Protectors—we remain justified in our defenses. Developing awareness of our choice empowers us with the inner knowing that there's an alternative path—that at any given moment, we can choose to turn inward. You can choose at this moment to accept that there's a plan to heal, and it begins with choice. We choose to pick up a book like this, we choose to go to therapy, we choose psychiatric support, meditation, holistic remedies—we choose to turn inward. Making that choice allows the ever-present energy of Self to take the lead, and the spiritual experience of genuine surrender can set in. You have the power to redirect your life right now by accepting this: your happiness is a choice you make; choice is a muscle, and the more often you choose to check in, the less time you'll spend checked out.

WHEN CHOICE FEELS FAR FROM REACH

I understand if you think it's ridiculous, irresponsible even, that I speak of happiness as just a choice away. "But I have real problems," you say. "And I can't choose to be happy when I live with all these issues." I get it. You might be struggling with addiction, depression, money worries, fear of violence, food insecurity, and countless other severe issues. Serious problems are not solved by choosing to be happy. Even right now reading about the power of choice may trigger a Protector part of you. Maybe you have a part that desperately needs to hold on to its beliefs and resists the idea that you have power to change.

I've experienced firsthand that in the darkest moments, choice is still possible. In 2019, I experienced suicidal postpartum depression. While this was the absolute worst time of my life, it also gave me the chance to understand mental illness on a personal level, and for this I'm grateful. At that time choosing to turn inward felt impossible, my meditation failed me, and I'd lost hope in my reality. But I never lost the ability to pray. Through a daily devotional prayer, I unconsciously made a choice—I chose to live. Although I didn't realize it at the time, prayer was the only choice I was capable of making. I chose to pray for help, I chose to pray for guidance, and while I resisted that guidance for several months, ultimately my prayers were answered. My choice to pray led me to get psychiatric support that ultimately saved my life. So while I wasn't able to choose happiness in that moment, the choice I made to pray and turn inward opened the door for Self to take the lead.

We can only experience the miracles we are willing to see. The miracle for me wasn't that I found a holistic way to end my suffering. The miracle was that I was able to see God and spirit in the guidance that led me to step into the psychiatrist's office and ultimately surrender to the safest healing path.

For me, prayer is nondenominational and rooted in my faith that there is a spiritual presence of support always guiding me. I recognize that even mentioning prayer could trigger some of your parts, especially if you have a conflicted history with religion or spirituality. If it's helpful, you can think of it as surrendering or setting an intention. (You can always feel free to adjust the spiritual or therapeutic lexicon throughout this book.) Consider this: when we pray, we pause and step back—momentarily surrendering our fears and concerns. A prayer is a way of asking for help—even if you don't know who you're asking. This slight adjustment, the moment of surrender, can offer relief to our parts.

PRAYER IS A WAY TO ASK FOR HELP

When I got sober at 25, my sponsor told me that the key to sobriety was to strengthen my faith in a Higher Power of my own understanding. At the time, I had no relationship to God or a Higher Power. But I admired my sponsor's sobriety and inner peace, so I was willing to follow her lead. "Fake it till you make it," she'd say. I loved this 12-Step slogan because it let me open my heart to possibility.

One afternoon during our weekly meetup, I hesitantly agreed to get on my knees and pray. Though I wasn't exactly sure who the heck I was praying to, I knew exactly what I was seeking. I prayed for help, for guidance and support.

Every single day from then on, I humbly got down on my knees and prayed, and you know what? It felt like a weight lifted off my shoulders. One day at a time, I found much-needed relief through prayer. I had the Serenity Prayer on repeat: "God grant me the serenity to accept the things I cannot change, the courage to change the things I can, and the wisdom to know the difference." I didn't know what God meant to me, but I did feel relief when I surrendered through prayer. The practice of turning to a Higher Power offered me relief throughout the day, giving me a moment to pause, surrender, and redirect.

I suggest you think of a prayer as a way to surrender and let go—it's like saying, "I'm flooded and I need some help." Each prayer is an act of surrender that can remind us of our ability to check in rather than remain checked out. The split second that we pause through prayer, we open an invisible door for Self energy to come forward and help soothe the Protectors. Each time we pray, we create a tiny bit of space between stimulus and reaction, allowing Self to come through. That split-second prayer can ignite curiosity, a tinge of compassion, or the commitment to turn inward. Prayer is a choice to see peace instead of fear.

Any time you've said or thought, "I can't go on like this" or "There has to be a better way," that's a prayer. The conscious desire for help is a prayer. Prayer opens our awareness to the possibility of choice, thereby activating Self energy inside. Each time we pray to "see peace instead of this," we surrender to a spiritual presence beyond our logic and reason. Turning inward is scary and often the last thing we want to do when we're triggered. In most cases it's not even a logical option because we've become so blended with the Protector that we can't see any other choice but to stay stuck managing our big feelings. But the more we pause and pray, the more aware we are of our power to choose to see through the lens of love instead.

WRITE YOUR STORY IN REAL TIME

A dear friend who also happens to be a spiritual coach once shared a valuable insight with me. She recounted an experience with a client who frequently used phrases like "I'm cursed" and "I feel like there's a perpetual dark cloud hanging over me." Her response to the client was profound: "When you repeat those words, you're writing your story in real time." It's a reminder that our beliefs create our reality, regardless of how challenging our circumstances may be. Each day we have the choice to rewrite the script of our life.

Take a moment to reflect on the power of your own choice. Your choice to read this book was a choice to turn inward and rewrite your story. To write a story filled with meaning. This isn't about reciting or affirming a new story that you don't truly believe in, it's about choosing to heal. Each time you pray, each time you choose to check in, you're sending a message to every part of you that you're willing to see through the lens of Self rather than the lens of fear.

There will be many times when you may be flooded, fearful, or blended with a Protector, and it may seem impossible to choose to check in. Take a moment to reflect on the times when you're so flooded that you forget that you have a choice. When does that happen? Maybe the moment you step into your childhood home, you totally lose your center, check out, and revert to childhood behavior. Perhaps every time you invest in yourself or spend money on personal needs, you find yourself overwhelmed by thoughts of financial insecurity. Or when the person you're newly dating doesn't text back right away, you freak out and feel like your world is over. Such states of disengagement can trap us in a narrative that we continuously revisit, like a repetitive loop. Once that loop builds up momentum, we believe it's our reality, forgetting that we had any other choice of how to think or feel. We become so stuck in repetitive Protector behavior and thoughts that choice is no longer an option we're consciously aware of.

The more extreme the Protector, the harder it is to remember that you can choose to check in. The Protector can be so flooded with emotions that its thoughts and beliefs become your ultimate truth. The thoughts we repeat become beliefs we carry, and what we believe, we create more of. The more stuck we are in the loop of the Protector's thoughts, the more chaotic and extreme our life can feel. This is where making choice a prayerful practice can help.

Consider each prayer a pivot inward toward Self—a conscious desire to heal. Each prayer is a momentary pause and a gentle reminder that you can choose again. When you're reminded of this choice, there's a strong chance you can begin to un-blend from the Protector (even for a moment).

Maybe you breathe a sigh of relief, or maybe you take the pressure off yourself for a split second, let go, and allow the spiritual presence of Self energy to enter into your subconscious. A prayer for Self-help invokes miraculous inner shifts.

A prayer is the choice to turn inward and get out of the loop. Prayer offers your Protectors hope that there is a gentler way to perceive your life. In that space you can sense the truth that your Protector *isn't you* but *a part of you*, and that it's safe to become more curious and open to what lies inside.

Exercising your choice to check in is not about willing yourself into a new belief system but instead starting with the acceptance that you have far more power than you think. It's a practice to remember this truth and a commitment to exercise it. Although you can often turn to choice quickly or even spontaneously in many situations, there will still be moments when certain parts can cause you to completely forget your choice, resulting in hours of delay before you return to it. What's important isn't the amount of time it takes to choose to check in; it's what happens inside you when you do. Allowing choice to lead you inward is a habitual shift in your mind and a neural adjustment in your brain.

PRAYER CHECK-IN

Adding prayer to the check-in process offers you a point of pivot. When choice feels far from reach, prayer can be the conduit to guide you back to remembering. Rather than overriding, ignoring, or even shaming the part, pray for choice. A simple prayer like "I choose to see peace instead of this" puts you right into the seat of Self. This prayer clears space for your check-in, allowing important information to be revealed.

Here's how I suggest you apply your prayer to the check-in process.

1. Begin by making prayer a habit. Each day when you notice a minor annoyance, a judgmental thought, or a sensation of inner criticism coming on, pause and pray: "I welcome help." This prayer invokes the power of your choice, sending a message inside that you're willing to receive guidance. When you make this prayer a daily habit (you can also use it throughout the day), it will become second nature to remember that you can ask for help.

   As you develop this pivot through prayer, you may begin to feel inspired to carry on with the check-in process. Remember, this prayer is enough to open up your consciousness to receive Good Orderly Direction—God. If you feel called to continue the check-in, take your next step.

2. When you notice a subtle sense of relief, it's time to **choose to check in** with your parts. Focus your attention inward, and allow the process to unfold.

3. Become **curious** and notice what feelings or sensations or thoughts come through. Be the nonjudgmental witness of your inner experience. What do you know about this part of you? In your journal give it space to respond.

4. **Compassionately connect** by asking the part what it needs right now. Listen and take it in. If you feel called, write out the response in your journal.

5. **Look for C qualities.** Place your hand on your heart and take a deep breath in. Notice inside for any of the C qualities of Self: calm, compassion, clarity, courage, creativity, connectedness, commitment. When you notice even the slightest sensation of a C quality of Self, place your hand on your heart and breathe. Breathe with Self and open your heart to receive more intuitive guidance. Don't push past this moment—this is the miracle when Self sets in. Sit for as long as you can in the presence of Self. To enhance this experience, I love to sit in meditation and feel the connection to Self in my body. To listen to the guided audio of this practice, go to DearGabby.com/SelfHelpResources.

Open your heart, be still, and let Self in.

PRESENCE AND PATIENCE

The power of the check-in process lies in your willingness to return to it over and over again. This process *is* a prayer; it's a conscious choice to turn inward for help. Checking in can become a habit that is stronger than your fear—with time and repetition the process becomes second nature, offering you a new way of relating to your inner world.

Consider the check-in process a daily devotional prayer that helps you grow and maintain a consistent connection with your parts. This connection is established through giving parts your attention, fostering curiosity, and cultivating a compassionate connection. The more frequently you employ these steps, the more ingrained they will become, making it easier for your protective parts to trust in the presence of your Self energy. This trust is the greatest love you'll ever know. It's a love that's unconditional, unwavering, and always available to you. This is the promise of choice.

It's important to emphasize the power of patience in your practice. As you open up to Self, more compassion can come through, which in turn allows for more patience with the process. Healing decades of Protectors won't happen overnight—remind yourself now that your Protectors have been running the show for so long. They've worked hard to keep you feeling safe, and you've grown to rely on their coping strategies. Consistent contact with your parts will allow space for Self. Be patient, knowing that miracles lie in the moment-to-moment shifts.

One prayer at a time welcomes Self into your awareness. There may be moments when you feel overwhelmed and find it challenging to initiate the process. In such instances, return to your prayer; if you don't feel an inner shift, that's fine. Trust that the shift is on the way. Maybe later that day you will find it easier to check in or experience a spontaneous moment of Self-awareness coming through. Prayer is the conduit for Self, and it will ignite your inner guidance, even if you don't feel it right away.

As you exercise your choice to turn inward one minute at a time, you're building a muscle within you. This muscle isn't fueled by judgment or rigidity; it's supported by compassion and calm. It becomes a constant presence, a steady guide that accompanies you through each challenge.

Be patient, knowing that the simplicity of choice is a guiding force on your journey. Your choice to check in holds the potential to reshape your perspective, your reactions, and ultimately your life. Remember, it's not about adhering to an intricate plan but about acknowledging the freedom within every moment. Notice the moments when you're able to be present with your parts, even for a split second. The presence you bring to your inner Protectors allows them to soften their edges. Presence lets parts know they are truly seen.

CHOICE GIVES YOU POWER WHEN YOU FEEL POWERLESS

An hour after I sat down to write this passage, I got my nails done. After years of pissing off nail techs in the salon, I finally found an amazing young man to do my nails. Vito and I spend an hour together every two weeks. This is an ongoing relationship that I am grateful to have manifested, not just for the lovely attention to my nails but for our deep and soulful conversation. Instead of scrolling on my phone or just tuning out, I enjoy the nail treatment while talking with Vito. His energy is so calm and open that it's easy for us to connect. At times he'll talk to me about his personal life or his career aspirations. Tonight he seemed a little down and I asked him about it. He shared with me that he was feeling "behind in life." Without hesitation I said, "The part of you that feels behind, how long has it been around?"

"Since I was a kid," he responded.

"Have you ever considered turning inward for guidance?"

His face relaxed and his energy softened. He said, "Just offering me that choice gives me hope."

CHAPTER 6

HOW YOU'LL KNOW SELF *IS* INSIDE

An IFS therapist friend of mine once said to me: "Gabby, I read your book *The Universe Has Your Back*, and within the first few paragraphs of the introduction I thought, 'She's speaking IFS.'" This comment came as a surprise because when I wrote that book I didn't even know about IFS. I was writing about my spiritual relationship and connection to my inner guidance system. The core message of that book is: transform fear into faith through spiritual connection.

Upon reflection I can see the clear through line between spirituality and the essence of IFS and how the primary tenets of IFS have been similar to my own spiritual path. Since my early 20s, I've devoted my life to healing the fear-based beliefs from my past through prayer, meditation, and inner spiritual development. Each time I'd notice a fearful thought or pattern, I'd say a prayer: "Thank you, guidance of the highest truth and compassion, for helping me transform this fear into love." Through my devotional spiritual practice, I would offer up my egoic, critical thoughts to the care of my inner guidance system—a spiritual presence of love and compassion—a Higher Power of my own understanding. Committing to the habit of witnessing my fear without judgment and offering it up to a Higher Power for healing *is* for me the essence of IFS. Day after day I'd invite a loving presence (Self) to enter into my mind and soothe my fearful perceptions of the world.

Self is an ever-present energy of love within us and around us. We all have Self energy available to us at all times. As we nurture and develop our connection to Self, we gain more access to it.

Clouding that access is the strong presence of our Protectors. None of us is exempt from constructing protective belief systems that trap us in unwanted patterns. Protectors take charge and influence our actions. However, as we nurture our inner world and embrace a spiritual connection to the energy of love, we can momentarily suspend our worldly beliefs and rediscover the Self that *is* inside. Healing occurs when we become willing to open our minds to new perspectives one shift at a time.

Even the slightest shift in perception from a Protector into Self is a miracle. I've had the honor of witnessing thousands of people experience a spiritual connection of their own understanding—an experience of Self. I've held space for some of the largest group meditations in the world and within minutes have felt the energy of a room full of thousands of people shift. I've guided guests on my podcast through the check-in process and within minutes witnessed the shift from extreme Protector anxiety to a Self-embodied calm. All that was required for these miracles was the slightest willingness to choose to turn inward for support.

By turning inward for support, we are blessed with Self-guidance and an inner experience of peace. The answers are inside because the outside search just doesn't work. There's nothing and no one outside us that can save us from the feelings inside. All the relief we look for in substances, relationships, success, and so on just isn't there. The relief is waiting for us inside. Your willingness to turn inward is all that is required. One subtle shift inward, one day at a time, allows you to remember that you're *not* alone, and that Self is there to help. In time you'll establish a connection to Self that you can rely on—an intuitive (spiritual) energy, an inner guidance system and sense of presence inside.

Each time you connect with a part, you take a brick down from the wall that blocks the presence of Self. The more committed you are to introspection, the more effortlessly these bricks come off. While this may make it seem like there's a long road ahead, I can assure you of one thing: there comes a moment when the divide between Self and your parts vanishes, granting you effortless access to the energy of love. The spiritual connection to Self has always been within you, and now is the moment to reclaim it.

MOLECULES OF SELF ARE ENOUGH

Each time you feel a molecule of Self energy enter in, you strengthen your faith that there's a loving presence inside. A molecule of connection will feel like a deep belly breath, a sigh of relief, a sensation of safety inside, an expansive feeling of presence, or even a spark of creative intuition. You'll experience any one (or more) of the C qualities of Self come through you naturally: compassion, courage, connectedness, calm, creativity, clarity, confidence, curiosity.

Self is the curiosity that guides you to turn the pages of this book. Self is coming through the energy I transmit through these pages. Self is the calmness you feel in meditation. Self is available to you right here and now. There's a heart-opening expansiveness inside as your Protectors settle and Self sets in. The presence of Self cracks you open to infinite possibilities. There is no place where you and Self don't intersect. It's in you, around you, and with you now. Feel my words, feel the energy coming through onto the page, and allow my Self energy to come through to you now.

Let Self in. I will continue to let Self write through me so you can experience the energy exchange. I truly believe that the energy I am expressing right now on this page is going to come through in every copy of this book. Remember, Self creates more Self.

BUILDING A NEW RELATIONSHIP

Reconnecting to Self is like reconnecting to an old friend. It can take time, but it can also happen spontaneously. The amount of time it takes to reestablish this connection is irrelevant; what matters most is your courage to turn inward. Once you do that, even the slightest molecule of Self energy is enough to strengthen your connection.

The more consciously you choose to connect to Self through the practices I'm sharing here, the easier it will be to experience presence and peace. As you develop more and more faith in Self, it will become a first responder guiding you to see the innocence in every part, allowing them all to soften.

Your connection to Self is the most profound relationship of your life. This is a relationship that will help you feel safe inside, thereby changing the way you experience the world. You will be able to live in the world but think and act with thoughts of love. You'll no longer be the victim of your past or future; rather, you'll be fully engaged in the present moment.

When a Protector part feels connected to Self (even for a slight moment), it can settle and release its grip. Again, I liken this connection to my daily experience with my six-year-old son, Oliver. When Ollie is flooded with emotions, instead of shutting him down, telling him "You're fine," or sending him into a time-out (big Gabby NO-NO), I'll do the opposite. I patiently check in with him and notice his feelings. Extending my Self energy to him, I'll say, "I see you're really mad right now." I'll get low on the floor and calmly ask, "Is there anything you want me to know about?" I remain curious and calm, allowing him to fully express his feelings. As soon as I notice his energy settle, his breath slow down, or his body relax, I'll compassionately connect: "What do you need right now? Do you need a hug?" Every time I extend this compassionate connection to him, I'm sending a powerful message to his brain—a message that his feelings matter, that it's perfectly safe to experience big emotions, and that I embrace every part of who he is.

Reflect on the profound significance of this connection for a child, and then imagine what it could mean for you to offer that same connection to your own inner parts. Contemplate the idea that by simply connecting your parts to Self, you are strengthening an inherent wisdom and inner guidance that you can faithfully rely on.

Surrendering to Self can be confronting because we've grown accustomed to not trusting. Take a moment to think of your childhood. Did you trust that your big feelings and emotions were safe to feel? Were your primary caregivers focused on your inner experience or instead on how you behaved—if you were a *good girl or boy*? Worse, were the people who were meant to care for you the source of your unsafety? Even if you had a strong attachment bond and positive upbringing, there were likely experiences that were not safe for your child brain to process. Without the proper support and processing, you were left alone to deal with your flooded emotions. Then, of course, a multitude of Protectors would arise to help you avoid ever facing the exiled pain and the core feelings of not being cared for.

But what if *you* could tend to those emotions now?

While a trusting connection to a caregiver may not have been available to you as a child, it's available to you now. The safe, secure, soothing parent you've always needed is right here, right now. I mean this. Just by picking up this book, you made a Self-guided choice; the courage to keep reading comes from the presence of Self inside you. Self is here now, you don't need to find Self, and you can release the blocks to the presence of Self that has always been there.

The Buddhist monk Thich Nhat Hanh said, "You calm your feeling just by being with it, like a mother tenderly holding her crying baby. Feeling the mother's tenderness, the baby will calm down and stop crying." When you can access your Self energy, it allows you to be there for your Protectors, giving them a feeling of security that helps them relax. You can stay present with your emotions, treating them with the same care you would offer to an innocent child—giving your parts a dependable and safe space within you.

SPONTANEOUS MOMENTS OF SELF

Throughout this journey you may experience spontaneous connections to Self. Maybe while practicing one of the journaling exercises, you notice a strong sense of curiosity come through, a curiosity so strong that it allows you to experience a new perspective. Or maybe, while you're practicing one of the meditations, peace and calm come over you. Keep your heart and mind open to connecting to Self. Remember, you don't have to access Self; you only need to release the blocks to the presence of Self energy within you.

When a part feels connected to Self, it can start to relax. The relaxation sets in because the young part of you feels like there's a trustworthy adult in the room. This trust usually takes time to build, but it can spontaneously show up if you're open to it. Dick Schwartz has a beautiful way of describing spontaneous connection to Self:

> We all know about those luminous moments of clarity and balance, in our own lives and in those of our clients, which come briefly now and again. However we get there, we suddenly encounter a feeling of inner plenitude and openheartedness to the world that wasn't there the moment before. The incessant nasty chatter inside our heads ceases, we have a sense of calm spaciousness, as if our minds and hearts and souls had expanded and brightened. Sometimes, these evanescent experiences come in a bright glow of peaceful certainty that everything in the universe is truly okay, and that includes us—you and me individually—in all our poor struggling, imperfect humanity. At other times, we may experience a wave of joyful connection with others that washes away irritation, distrust, and boredom. We feel that, for once, we truly are ourselves, our real selves, free of the inner cacophony that usually assaults us.[1]

I experience the luminous moments of Self when I'm giving a motivational talk. When I'm speaking I can get out of my head, attune to the spirit within me, and harness a transformational source of energy—Self energy. I can get into the flow, allow words to come through me, and feel the greatest experience of presence. I feel connected, inspired, and alive. Does this sound familiar? Have you ever experienced a great sensation of expansiveness while exercising, or creative energy while making art? Maybe you've noticed the calmness of Self come through after a deep meditation. Take note of the times in your life when you spontaneously experience this type of relief.

I experienced such a spontaneous moment recently with a caller on my podcast, *Dear Gabby*. I'm in the recording studio and I bring randomly selected guests onto a screen to take questions and coach them in real time (hence Dear Gabby). As soon as this particular guest got on the screen, I had a sense that she needed to check in. Her Protector was stuck in the cycle of self-criticism. She kept referring to an "inner critic" that was running the show, keeping her small, and holding her back from what she desired in life. But in just five minutes I guided her to choose to check in, become curious, and compassionately connect. Her openness allowed her to swiftly turn inward, and it was easy for her to notice the part. When we got to the connection step, I asked her, "How do you feel toward this inner critic part of you?" She immediately responded, "I feel compassion for her. My heart is open and all I feel is love." Tears welled up in her eyes. The moment I heard the word *compassion* come through, I knew that Self was in the room.

This fast connection to Self was a major catalyst for my guest. Her entire energy shifted. Then I asked, "What does the part need?" She responded, "More of this." She left our conversation with a whole new energy and outlook on her life.

Several months later she was again picked at random to come back on the podcast as a guest. "Do you remember me, Gabby? I'm the woman who had a serious inner critic that was running my life."

"Yes, my love! How are you?"

"Well, the inner critic is still alive and outspoken, but it no longer has such a hold on me. In our brief encounter, I had a major shift! I was able to see the inner critic as a young part of me, rather than *as* me. I felt compassion for it—and I've been able to access that compassion often."

In just a few minutes during a live recording of my podcast, this woman experienced a radical shift that changed her forever. It's not that the inner critic disappeared, but that she was able to experience the inner critic differently—with compassion. This spontaneous connection to Self was so eye-opening for her that it offered a whole new way of relating to the inner critic. She no longer got sucked into the storyline (at least most of the time she didn't) and instead was able to be the witness of the inner critic as a part of her. Through that lens, Self-compassion set in.

CHECK IN AND MEDITATE

Let's take a moment for an experience of Self. This grounding check-in process adds a 90-second breath-based meditation that will offer you a chance to tap into the sensations of Self energy. If you feel called to check in now, then follow my guidance. To listen to the guided audio of this practice, go to DearGabby.com/SelfHelpResources.

Choose to check in by focusing your attention inward, attuning to any parts that may be present at this time.

Ground your energy in this step with an affirmation to invoke Self: "I welcome the calm energy of Self to enter into this gentle process."

Extend curiosity inward by checking in with any thoughts, feelings, or sensations inside. If you notice a part come forward, give it your attention. Be present with what comes through. Just spend a little time with the part and allow it to reveal whatever needs to come through.

Stay present and curious.

Next extend **compassionate connection** through a 90-second meditative breath practice.

Find a comfortable seated position cross-legged on the floor or upright in a chair. Gently close your eyes.

Once again notice the part that's with you now. Notice any tension in your body, any pain, or emotional distress.

Identify where these feelings and sensations are in your body.

Place your hand on that space in your body.

Take a deep breath in and feel into the feeling, whether physical or emotional, and breathe in and out with it for 90 seconds.

Breathe into the feeling the part holds.

If it's in your chest, breathe into your chest, and on the exhale let it go.

If it's tension in your neck, breathe into that tension, and on the exhale let it go.

If it feels like an overwhelming sensation of sadness, breathe into the sadness, and on the exhale let it go.

Breathe deeply into the feeling, offering it a chance to truly express its emotions or pain.

Then gently let that go.

Breathe in and feel all the feelings, emotions, and sensations.

Breathe out and let it go.

Continue this cycle of breath for 90 seconds.

If you feel called to continue this breath longer, go for it. Let Self guide you.

Check for C qualities of Self. Offering the part more presence, now just notice if you feel a sensation of calmness. Do you feel a connection in your heart? Are you aware of any sensations of compassion, clarity, creativity? Take a moment to notice if any C qualities of Self have come forward.

Be present with the sensations of Self. Gently keep your eyes closed and tap into whatever sensations and feelings arise. There's no right or wrong emotion. Just notice what you notice. At this moment are you aware that there is a loving presence inside? Are you aware that Self is with you now?

Spend some time breathing into these new sensations. Open your heart to receive more connection and an inner sense of compassion. Breathe in deeply and exhale completely. Spend some time marinating in the energy of Self. When you feel ready, return to this chapter.

This 90-second breathing practice has proven to be invaluable to me for more than 20 years. In the early days of my sobriety, I grappled with an extremely vigilant Protector part that was constantly on edge. During that period I was discovering the power of using my breath to ease my anxiety. The straightforward method of recognizing the sensation of anxiety within my body and then intentionally breathing into that sensation for 90 seconds was transformative. Each instance where I would take a moment to acknowledge my anxious feelings and breathe through them, I found myself feeling more serene and grounded. At the time I didn't know that this breathing technique was a form of connecting with Self. Today I can see that Self was available to me through my breath, even amid that challenging time. Incorporate this mindful breathing into your own check-in practice as a way of strengthening your somatic experience of Self. Allow this meditative check-in to help you begin to truly feel Self inside.

THE MIRACLE OF SELF

My spiritual practice has taught me that the definition of a miracle is a shift in perception—a shift from fear to love. When teaching the check-in process and the principles of IFS, I've witnessed many miracle moments. One particularly astounding transformation using the check-in process took place during one of my sessions at the residential addiction center. It was nothing short of a miracle. As I entered the auditorium, on my way to the stage, I noticed a young woman in the audience. She sat in her chair, leaning back with her head tilted to the side and her eyes rolled back. Her arms were crossed, shutting off any connection to the rest of the people in the room. Her posture, facial expression, and energy seemed to resemble that of an addict drifting into unconsciousness.

Stepping onto the stage, I began my talk by recounting my personal sober journey starting at age 25. I shared how I transformed my relationship to addiction. I explained that through IFS I now see that the addict part of me once served as a shield against confronting unbearable traumatic memories. I expressed gratitude for my addict part, acknowledging the role it played in protecting me from exiled trauma.

By sharing my story, I established a safe and compassionate space to introduce the essential concepts of the check-in process. I explained Exiles and Protectors. Then I asked the audience, "What parts are in the room with you right now?"

The community began calling out parts: "Rage is in the room." "Shame." "Fear." "Judgment." "Guilt." Then, from the corner of the audience, I heard a young woman speak up—the same young woman I had noticed on my way into the room—and say, "I'm checked out." I looked at her with love and compassion and said, "I get that. I have a part of me that checks out too."

Once the group established some awareness of a part inside, I led them through a meditation to help them connect to the part. I helped them check in and honor the feelings, sensations, and thoughts that were coming forward. Then I slowly helped them become more curious about the part inside with questions like "Is there an age, gender, story, or image?" Then I asked them to place one hand on their heart and their other hand on their stomach and ask, "How can I help you? What do you need right now?" I guided the audience to notice the feelings and sensations in their bodies and move their hand on the place where they felt the most discomfort. For 90 seconds the group shared the experience of breathing into the feelings and sensations of their parts.

I noticed that the young woman who had been slouching was now sitting up straight. Her hand was on her heart and tears were flowing from her eyes. Her face looked different. She was serene, released, at ease. Her posture had changed, her jaw was relaxed, and I saw an auric glow around her as the tears continued to flow down her face.

I finished the meditation and asked the group to slowly open their eyes, and after a moment of stillness, I invited them to share their experience. The young woman raised her hand and said, "I've never felt safe in my entire life until just now. When I put my hand on my heart, my whole body settled. I heard an inner voice tell me I am safe." Tears flowed from my eyes as I witnessed the miraculous shift in her mind, body, and spirit. It was as if she'd had an awakening. Her heart was open to the wounded, exiled child part inside, the Protector who'd been checking out throughout her life—checking out in an effort to avoid facing its wounds. This meditative connection to Self offered her the first experience of inner safety she had ever known.

When the talk was over, the young woman walked toward the stage to speak to me. As I watched her approach, I was shocked to see how her physical and energetic presence had shifted. She looked like a totally different person. She looked young and innocent and unburdened. Her eyes were filled with relief and her heart was open. We embraced. As I held her in my arms, I heard her say, "This is a turning point for me. This sense of safety has offered me hope." Her connection to Self, even for just a moment, held the possibility to redirect her life.

THE SENSATION OF SELF

When you have an experience of Self, you get a taste of what's possible. Each time you pay close attention to your physical sensations and subtle inner experiences without trying to immediately resolve or change them, you can give your Protectors space to adjust naturally. When you begin to embody more Self, your inner dialogue changes, your body feels open, and your heart expands. This connection inward offers you a deeper connection to your Protectors and clarity about what they're signaling to you. By consciously contacting your Protector through the meditative check-in process, you'll establish an inner sensation signaling that Self is inside. With every gentle inner inquiry, you establish more and more wholeness inside.

Choosing Self through the check-in process is a practice that you can bring with you everywhere. I have a ritual prior to stepping on stage. I check in to see if any parts are present at the moment—maybe a controlling part that doesn't like the lighting setup—or a young child part that's upset about the way my hair was styled. Instead of bringing these parts out onstage with me, I welcome Self in to help. Using the meditation from this chapter, I breathe into the feelings and sensations for 90 seconds. Then I invoke the energy of Self through prayer: "Thank you, energy of the highest truth and compassion, for speaking through me." The meditative check-in gives my Protectors the attention they need, and the prayer welcomes Self to join me onstage. This preshow ritual allows me to feel the energy of Self move through me when I walk onto the stage, like invisible angel wings behind me. Words beyond my own come through, a tingling sensation moves through my extremities, time stops, and love flows. I feel connected, compassionate, and courageous. This creative connection to Self is one of the most profound feelings I know.

SELF IS AVAILABLE TO YOU NOW

Reflecting on this feeling connects me to Self energy as I type these words. I feel the calm sensation of Self settle into my nervous system. I have a mellow Spotify mix playing in the background. My son is asleep in the other room. The lights are dim, the curtains are closed. I'm in a safe, comfortable bed. A blue butterfly charm sits on my bedside table. I feel spiritually aligned, inspired, and connected to Self. I can let go and allow my brain to shift gears, step aside from the logic, the outline, the lessons. I can be an untethered force of light.

My hope is that as you read my words, you feel the energy of Self come off the page. I hope you feel my connection to you. We have a lot in common, you and I. We are seekers, looking for grace, inner peace, and a fearless way of life. The freedom we desire is available to us when we tend to our parts and help them settle. When we do that, we become quiet inside. In silent stillness we receive the inner wisdom, love, and connection we need most. We let Self in.

Open your heart to this new way of living and put your faith in this plan. A simple path of turning inward for wisdom beyond your logic and reason. A path that offers you miracles. Stay open, receptive, and curious. Relish every encounter with Self.

Let me offer you some of this Self energy now with a prayer:

May you feel compassion toward yourself. May you open your heart to all of your Parts. May you experience the sensation of presence inside. May you have faith in Self.

CHAPTER 7

ANXIOUS PARTS

I'm no stranger to anxiety. I've experienced the all-encompassing terror coursing through my nervous system like a live wire. I know the perpetual cycle of panic, overwhelming fear, and the inability to be in the present. The sleepless nights and the early hours watching the sun rise without having had a minute of sleep. It's that terrifying sense that the anxiety will never subside, accompanied by the constant urge to numb, control, and distract from the unbearable feelings.

For nearly four decades, I lived with an undiagnosed anxiety disorder. I controlled it with daily meditation, therapy, yoga, and every kind of holistic healing method. While these practices offered momentary relief, they never actually addressed the root cause, and eventually the anxiety started to win. Two months after giving birth to my son, I began to experience extreme anxiety that turned into insomnia, panic attacks, and suicidal ideation. Instead of turning inward and becoming curious about the anxiety—giving it space to reveal what it truly needed—I pushed it down, did a spiritual bypass around it, used medicinal herbs and acupuncture, and sought everything possible to avoid facing the reality that my anxiety needed my *attention*, not an herbal remedy.

The anxious part of me that I'd been managing for so long could no longer hide now, because the biochemical conditions and the extreme triggers of feeling out of control as a new mother made the anxiety impossible to manage. After months living from Protector to Protector and overriding the anxiety with external actions and behaviors, I finally had no other choice but to turn inward, surrender, and seek professional help.

I remember the day I hit bottom. I hadn't slept the night before—not for one minute. On that morning, my therapist gave me a call and told me, "It's time for me to step in." She proceeded to inquire about the anxious part, using the familiar series of IFS questions she had asked me dozens of times before. This time, though, there was a noticeable shift. I had reached a point where I could let go of my protective mechanisms and truly connect with my anxiety. When she asked, "What does this anxious part need?" I didn't hesitate; I replied, "It needs help." These three words became the catalyst for my journey toward healing.

In retrospect I can see that there was another part in the way of me facing and caring for the anxiety. That part was shame. The shame of my postpartum mental illness kept me from getting help sooner. Mental illness produces defensive parts that oftentimes override the anxious and depressed parts that need our attention. In my case, the shame part nearly took my life.

I was incredibly resistant to the idea that I could be dealing with a mental illness. It was difficult to acknowledge that despite having access to numerous resources, I struggled to navigate the postpartum period. I can see now how shame took months of my life away from me and kept me from the early days of bonding with my son. Thankfully I hit enough of a bottom to let a glimmer of Self-connection come through—the connection that helped me soothe the shame and accept the psychiatric support I truly needed.

My story reveals that when we offer our anxious parts a connection to Self, they can open up to greater possibilities for healing. In my case, the IFS inquiry helped me calm the anxiety enough to see through the clouds and open up to the support of an SSRI. This medication was a means to address the biochemical response to postpartum depression, establishing a foundation of inner stability that would enable me to embark on the deeper IFS work necessary for healing the root cause of my condition: the Exile.

The all-encompassing nature of anxiety can be very hard to pierce, especially when one suffers from a biochemical condition. Some biochemical conditions we're born with; others arise from PTSD. In many cases medication offers us inner safety on the path toward deeper therapeutic healing.

In my own experience, I can confidently say that I've benefited greatly from antidepressants, but the pills were just part of the solution. Medication provided me with a glimpse of what safety could feel like. It gave me years of living in a new state of peace, enabling my brain to forge new neural pathways. It offered me a sense of safety within my body. Yet throughout this time, I remained aware that beneath the medication lay a live wire of anxiety that needed my support. It needed my curiosity and compassionate connection. It needed Self. While medication offered me the bridge to relief, long-lasting healing required that I take the necessary therapeutic steps toward deeper recovery. So whether you're medicated for anxiety or not, even more relief is available to you when you choose to check in and let Self help the part.

ANXIETY DESERVES OUR ATTENTION

Anxiety is a sensation that is all-encompassing, a physical and somatic response, a persistent thought with a hidden objective: safeguarding you from unveiling deeper exiled wounds. It's an extreme Protector that affects our health, sleep, relationships, aspirations, and overall well-being. Anxiety is on high alert, ready to distract from any Exiles that become activated. For many of us, it can feel safer to focus on the anxiety than to let it go, because unconsciously we fear what lies beneath it.

At times, when dormant Exiles resurface, the fear, trauma, and shame can be too overwhelming to confront. Anxiety often becomes the first responder, sweeping in with intense physical and emotional discomfort—sufficient to veil the underlying, deeper suffering of the exiled parts. The feeling of anxiety can become all-encompassing, overriding other parts to protect against facing deeper wounds. The anxious Protector takes over your mind and body, making it impossible to focus on anything else.

An example of this is my friend Sasha, whom I visited while her mother was in town. "It must be nice to have your mother here helping out with the kids," I commented.

"Actually, I'm crawling out of my skin. Being around her makes me unbearably anxious," Sasha replied, her tone shifting. She described how her mother could be kind one moment and then inexplicably lash out at her the next. "This unpredictability was my entire childhood. I never knew which version of my mom would appear. It's no surprise I developed an anxiety disorder."

Sasha's story unveiled the roots of her hypervigilant anxiety—being perpetually on guard—protecting her against the erratic behavior of her mother. Her anxiety served as a means to stay prepared for whatever her mother might do next. Moreover, it provided a distraction, a focal point away from the deeper pain of a fractured emotional bond with her mother. By witnessing our anxieties through this new lens, we do more than just alleviate symptoms; we shine light on the parts of ourselves that live beneath the anxiety.

A shift can set in if you open your heart to perceive your anxiety as a Protector part rather than a feeling you can't avoid. When I chose to see my anxiety as a Protector, I was able to stop pushing against it and start to connect to it. Initially, addressing your anxious parts might appear worrisome. The worried part of you may be concerned that paying attention to anxiety could exacerbate it. However, I've discovered that the opposite is true. Rather than resisting anxiety, which often intensifies it, you can observe it as a Protector part that needs your attention. Wholeheartedly embracing an anxious part as it is and allowing it room to exist can offer it instant relief.

Healing anxiety involves a multifaceted approach that necessitates Self's guidance. What's essential is a conscious commitment to regularly connecting with the anxious part by approaching it with compassion and curiosity. This approach allows the anxious part to feel seen, soften, and reveal its genuine needs.

After my postpartum diagnosis, it became clear to me that I'd lived with extreme, debilitating anxiety for most of my life. Managing anxiety left me feeling helpless, sick, and like a hamster on a wheel replaying the same experience day over day. I was so blended with the anxious Protector that I had no idea there was another way to live. No one ever taught me that my anxiety was the effect of deeper wounds; I was just left with it.

Most often people are so blended with their anxious part that they believe there's no way out of it. Our Protector parts have built up such strong roles inside our internal system that we no longer feel there can be any other way. We take on the roles of our Protectors as if they define who we are. We believe we're anxious people and that's just the way it is. Our parts have accepted their extreme roles and believe that if they stop doing what they're doing, they will be in great danger. Parts hold on so tightly to their roles that the idea of doing anything differently can be terrifying.

WE ALL HAVE ANXIOUS PARTS

It's hard to be alive and be immune to anxiety. All you have to do is look at your phone and you'll instantly be flooded with cortisol. A few months back, my friend introduced me to an app that tracked stress levels. It had a gamification element where you could test your levels by watching a scale on the app. If you got into the red zone of the scale, it meant your stress was rising. If you were connected to your breath and consciously relaxing, you'd see the scale turn green. I tested it out and was blown away by the results. For the first 30 seconds, I was able to stay in the green zone, regulating my nervous system by breathing deeply and exhaling completely. Then I saw a notification on my phone. The second I shifted my attention to turning off the notification, the scale went red—really red! In a split second I went from Zen calm to extreme anxiety. I was amazed by how quickly my physiology responded to the simple act of turning off a phone notification. From that point forward, I became mindful of the shift in my feelings each time I turned to my phone. This newfound awareness offered me the chance to see how much stress our phones can add to our lives.

Modern life is full of these daily stressors, and most people don't have any awareness of how to ease them. That's why I believe this will be the chapter you return to over and over again. My hope is to offer you a process for relating to your anxiety in a whole new way. Whether you have access to therapeutic support or not, you have Self. Follow the steps and let Self help your anxious part.

BEFRIENDING ANXIETY

I once addressed an audience of 2,000 people and asked if they had experienced anxiety in the past week. A resounding *yes* flooded the room. I then asked them to share their feelings about their anxiety. Their responses included "Frustrated." "Afraid." "Angry." "Annoyed." "Terrified." As I listened to their responses, I noticed an energy of connection take over the room. We were all speaking for a part that in some way had meaningfully affected our lives. A room full of strangers had a shared connection. Inside myself I noticed my heart open to the group as a compassionate, connected energy began to pour through me. "You're not alone, my friends. Feel the connection in the room right now. We're all in this together." Words of compassion began to flow out of me: "I understand your suffering and I honor your experience. I know how scary it's been to not know how to help your anxious parts. Once again, feel into the connection in this room. Our anxiety is speaking to us; it wants to get our attention. Let's all take a moment now to close our eyes, focus our attention inward, and offer our anxiety some space to speak for what it needs."

Following this channeled flow, I led the group in this guided practice of checking in with the anxious part:

Focus your attention inward and find where the anxiety lives in your body.

Then place your hand on that part of your body, offering it your attention.

Notice the feelings and sensations. Is there a tightness, or pain? Is there a color associated with it?

Take a moment to breathe deeply into the feeling or sensation of the anxiety. Then breathe out.

Connecting more now, feel more deeply into the feeling of anxiety. Breathe into the feeling and exhale completely.

Breathe in.

Breathe out.

Breathe in through your nose.

Breathe out.

Give your anxious part more breath for one more minute.

Upon completing this spontaneous Self-led meditation, I asked the group to gently open their eyes. "What do you feel like now?" I called out.

Self qualities now filled the room; "I feel relief." "Freedom." "Expansiveness." "Compassion." "Connectedness." "Calm."

In a three-minute meditation, a group of 2,000 people shifted their perception from fearing their anxiety to befriending it. They shifted from feeling isolated to feeling connected. From frustrated with their anxiety to compassionate toward it. The creative energy of Self moved me to share this meditation, which in turn activated the Self-healing energy of the group. The meditation offered a way for them to see their anxiety through the lens of compassion and a practice they could turn to for the rest of their lives. This practice of checking in with their anxiety and compassionately connecting to it meant they no longer needed to fear it. With a tool for relief in their pocket, they no longer felt controlled by their anxiety but instead were in relationship with it.

I want to offer this miraculous shift to you now. What if you could befriend your anxiety instead of fighting against it?

CHECK IN WITH YOUR ANXIOUS PART

If you're open to exploring this perspective, let's take a moment to check in. Gently turning your attention inward, see if there's even a little willingness to give your anxiety some attention. If you find it comfortable to embrace the idea that your anxiety might be a Protector part, and if you're willing to work with it, I encourage you to proceed with the anxiety check-in process. However, if for any reason this feels triggering or overwhelming, I suggest you just read this section and hold off on practicing the steps. You can always return to it when you feel ready.

You'll see that in this specific check-in process, I've added some anxiety-related elements to the steps you're already familiar with. These additional steps can be applied when working with any part, but I recommend paying special attention to them when you're checking in with an anxious part. To listen to the guided audio of this practice, go to DearGabby.com/SelfHelpResources.

GIVE YOURSELF A SAFE BASELINE

Anxiety often has us in a headlock so tight that we cannot remember we have the choice to check in. With that in mind, I suggest that your first step is to establish a sense of safety.

The fastest way to offer your anxiety a baseline of safety is through your breath. Stanford neuroscientist Andrew Huberman teaches a five-second breathing technique to reduce anxiety and stress. If you ask someone with anxiety to just take a deep breath and relax, their response might be something like "Yeah, right, nice try!" Maybe you're having that response right now. Instead of skipping this step, give me just two breaths and we can create a new baseline of calmness in your system. When you're anxious or stressed, your breath becomes shallow, and at times it can even feel like you're suffocating. This breath practice can be very supportive because it activates the body's relaxation response, which is the opposite of the stress response.

When you're stuck in an anxiety attack or your breathing is shallow and distressed, it can be hard to even choose to check in with the part. That's why I've chosen to begin this specific check-in process with your breath.

Here's how it works:

- Take two quick breaths in through your nose, inhaling fast.
- Then breathe out slowly through your mouth with a complete exhalation.
- Practice this breath pattern at least twice, and continue longer if it feels supportive.

Once you notice a sense of calm relief or a deeper, more connected breath pattern, you'll know you're ready for the next step.

CHOOSE TO CHECK IN BY ASKING THE ANXIOUS PART FOR PERMISSION

Before you begin the check-in process, ask your anxiety for permission to check in. Anxiety is an extreme part that can feel overwhelming to face. Choosing to check in with your anxiety can feel scary and might invite more Protectors into the process. So I suggest that you be gentle, go slow, and ask permission. Ask your anxious part if it's okay to check in. If the answer is no, continue with the breath practice until you feel a stronger sense of safety. Then, you can ask the anxious part if it wants to check in. (It's okay if you just breathe and don't move on to the check-in process at all. Do what feels best inside you.)

Curiosity. Ask the anxious part this series of questions:

- What feelings, thoughts, or sensations are present?
- How long has your anxiety been around?
- What triggers it?
- What does it fear will happen if you let it go?
- If it wasn't in this extreme role of anxiety, what else might it be doing?
- Is there anything else it wants you to know? Spend as much time as you need getting to know this anxious part.

Compassionately connect. Now take a moment to place one hand on your heart and your other hand on your belly and compassionately create connection. Ask the anxious part, "What do you need right now?"

Listen to the part as it reveals whatever is needed in this moment. If at any point in this process you start to feel stuck, simply ask the part why it feels stuck. The process is led by your willingness to stay curious. Remember, parts are like little children: once you get them talking, they continue to open up. Give this anxious part permission to speak up and share whatever it needs.

CHECK FOR C QUALITIES OF SELF

Take a moment to reflect on how you feel toward your anxiety now. Do you notice that you're softer toward it? Do you feel any sensations of calmness? Is there a glimmer of compassion now that you know more about your anxiety? What C qualities (compassion, connection, clarity, creativity, calmness, courage, curiosity, confidence) do you notice? Take note of any C qualities that have come through, and honor the Self energy that is available to you now. Open your journal and take some time to write about your experience. Writing about any sensation or connection to Self energy is powerful because the next time you feel paralyzed by anxiety, you can reread your journal and remember that Self is always there to help.

GET INTO RELATIONSHIP WITH YOUR ANXIETY

Anxiety serves as a common Protector in most of our lives, often blending so seamlessly with our existence that we come to believe it will never go away. So I recommend prioritizing regular check-ins with your anxious part. By consistently making these check-ins, you'll offer it the attention it needs and way to interrupt the pattern of anxiety.

Chances are, anxiety has fulfilled a protective role in your inner world for as long as you can remember. Keep in mind that anxiety swiftly responds to any triggers from your repressed past, redirecting your focus away from those inner Exiles and onto an overwhelming physical sensation. The process of unraveling the anxiety response requires commitment and practice. However, as you start to experience the relief it offers, you'll naturally gravitate toward more of it, and the practice will become second nature.

Incorporating this practice into my morning routine, soothing my anxiety from the very beginning of the day, enabled me to begin each day with a calm spirit and an open heart—a connection to Self—and allowed my other Protectors to relax as well. Regardless of how busy my mornings were, I discovered that I had increased energy and enhanced focus. I could prepare my son for school effortlessly and be more affectionate toward my husband. Starting my day without anxiety significantly reduced my son's morning stress as well. Children are always co-regulating with our energy and our parts, so when my anxious part was at ease, Ollie felt more settled and his own anxious part remained dormant. The same positive impact extended to my coworkers. I found myself more patient and relaxed, allowing others the chance to feel calm too. All because I started my day by befriending my anxious part. A great way to set yourself up with Self energy at the onset of your morning is to practice the anxious parts meditation. To listen to the guided audio of this practice, go to DearGabby.com/SelfHelpResources.

I had so much success checking in with my anxiety in the morning that I started to practice it all throughout the day. It's become such a natural part of my routine that I check in automatically now. During a work call, I'll notice when I'm holding my breath, a sign that my anxious part has taken the stage. At those moments, I'll just take a deep breath and tune in. It's a quick, subtle process that goes unnoticed by others. I swiftly shift my focus inward and cultivate a sense of compassionate connection. I've honed the ability to self-regulate in the moment and return to a state of inner calm. It doesn't happen every time, but when it does, it's miraculous.

Even in extreme cases when my anxious Protector is on high alert, I still have the mindful awareness that I can check in with it. What previously would have taken me a week of overriding my anxious part now takes less than an hour. I have enough awareness and connection to the somatic experience of this part that I can choose to check in far faster than ever before.

If you find that checking in with your anxiety brings you relief, I strongly recommend making it a regular practice. Keep returning to this process again and again. Don't underestimate the profound impact of redirecting your attention inward and compassionately asking your anxious part to reveal its needs. These parts are remarkably wise and tend to open up when given the chance. Providing your anxiety with the space to breathe and connecting with it somatically is a potent method for slowing down the stress response and calming your nervous system. And once you sense even the slightest relief, extend some compassionate connection to your anxious part.

The more I practice these steps, the less fearful I am of my anxiety. I now know how to calm my nervous system, settle down, and compassionately check in with the anxious parts that arise inside me. Knowing that I have a tool to soothe my anxiety has offered me the freedom to live and trust that there is a way through every anxious block. With this practice, I am no longer the victim of my anxiety; instead I can connect to it and offer it the presence of Self. I know and trust that whenever my anxious parts arise, Self can help.

SELF IS ALWAYS THERE TO HELP

I recently saw a quote from a preacher that said, "All your children want from you is your unconditional love." The same goes for parts. Without our curiosity and attention, parts stay stuck in their undesirable roles, managing our lives and putting out fires. But when we get into the check-in process and start to ask the parts what they need instead of overriding their suffering, parts feel loved and respected. They want to be loved unconditionally, and that is what Self offers. While at first these Self-loving moments of connection may be brief, they are profound. Each time a Protector part senses Self energy, your inner system and your brain have a new experience. An experience of unconditional love. This process creates new neural pathways and a new way of perceiving yourself. Your trust in the brief encounters with Self is enough to set transformational, long-lasting change in motion.

Connecting to the presence of Self allows our anxious parts to become clear and empowered in knowing that there's a way out of the suffering—the way out is to go in. When we establish any form of connection to our anxious parts, we can see them differently. So much of our fear of anxiety stems from the fear of not knowing how to make it stop. When we accept that we don't have to stop it, but can instead connect to it, we can receive great clarity from Self.

Protector parts are attached to their roles and in many ways rely on them to stay "safe." But when you give the parts some attention, healing becomes possible. If even for a moment you calmly check in with the Protector, the possibility for relief can set in. I want you to know that hope is always possible and Self is always there to help. In times of crisis it can feel impossible to connect to Self, which is why it's so important to make Self-help a practice. The more you apply the principles of Self-help, the more you'll learn to rely on Self to be there, especially in your darkest hour.

If at any point you feel overwhelmed by an anxious part, consider checking in and trying this: dog-ear this page of the book and return to it whenever you're in an extreme moment of anxiety. Place your hand on your heart, take a deep breath in, and allow the Self energy in my words to soothe you.

Hello, my friend. I'm here, I'm with you, and I see you. Take a deep breath in and release. Continue this cycle of breath as you connect to my words. In this moment you can let my words be your guide. Trust that the power of Self can be transferred through this page. Feel into my calm presence. Notice my loving energy come through this page energetically. Let my Self energy come through for you now. I am here to remind you that you're not alone. You are connected to me and to all the other people reading this book. Your anxious part just wants to give you some information and get your attention. By gently offering it your slightest breath, you can let Self help you feel calm. I am proud of your courage to read this passage and your clarity that there is help inside. By reading my words, you are welcoming Self to help you now. You are not alone. Self energy is here with you right now. You have this connection inside you, and you allow each sentence to remind you of this. Breathe in deeply and exhale completely. I am consciously infusing these words with Self energy, and I trust the flow of energy is coming through on this page. You are safe, you are seen, and you are loved and connected to the ever-present energy of Self. You are not alone.

I hope this passage offers you a sense of connection, compassion, and calmness. If it supports you, I suggest you return to it.

Each time you offer your anxious part the chance to check in with the steps, you're sending it a message that Self can help. The more you check in, the safer your anxious part will feel and the more it will trust that Self can help. Pay attention to the moments of relief, allowing each slight connection to Self energy to act as spiritual proof that you are guided. We become clear and empowered in knowing that there's a way out of our suffering—the way out comes from checking in.

THE COURAGE TO HEAL

When I was finishing up this chapter, I was five days into the process of titrating down on my anxiety medication and felt secure in pursuing the plan my psychiatrist had laid out for me. I fully acknowledge that stopping medication does not work for everyone; for many people, relying on medication for support is crucial and indispensable. In my case, over the four years following my postpartum anxiety diagnosis, I greatly benefited from the support of an SSRI. At a certain point, it made sense for me to discontinue the medication. However, I didn't rush the process. Instead I allowed the medication to create a foundation of safety so that I could embark on the deeper therapeutic journey of connecting with the Exiles that my anxiety had concealed for so long. My dedication to understanding my parts and strengthening my trust in Self established a new baseline of inner safety, instilling a belief that I could gradually and gently reduce my medication with the guidance of a psychiatrist and my inner trust in Self.

It's not a coincidence that five days into the tapering process, I found myself working on this chapter. I believe it was divine spiritual guidance and a gentle reminder that the Universe has my back when I'm aligned with Self. I could sense the Self energy that it took to let go of the support of the SSRI and make this big change in my life. I recognized the Self-led **courage** that gave me the faith to begin the process. I was **clear** about the importance of proceeding with this process gradually. It was crucial to give myself ample time—perhaps as much as a year—to titrate, allowing for Self energy to support me. I'm grateful for the heightened **connection** to my internal system that offered me cues for when I needed to slow down or ask for help. My access to the **calm** energy of Self was always ready for me the moment I tuned in to my breath. Each step of the check-in process was there to hold me up as I titrated down. I felt **confident** that I could navigate the journey safely, and my anxious part was filled with hope, knowing that I was guided by Self.

CHAPTER 8

BODY PARTS

"What's wrong?" I ask, staring at my husband as we make our way to Thanksgiving dinner at my in-laws'. He's in the driver's seat, his brow furrowed and shoulders tense.

"My back hurts," he replies.

This is a common exchange between us. I have a part that is hypervigilant about Zach's well-being, often attempting to manage his emotions in order to regulate my own. On the other hand, Zach has a part that brings him considerable discomfort, a part that truly runs his show: back pain.

As I write this, I can already imagine him reading this for the first time. I'm aware that this particular example might piss him off. My instinct is to delete it and start over. Yet instead of avoiding his reaction, what if I write this chapter *for* him? And not just for him but for all of us—for every person struggling with any form of chronic pain or condition.

I sit with it and hear an inner voice say, "Go for it, Gabby, write it for his back, write it for your jaw, write it for all the physical Protector parts that need a new perspective." I embrace the inner message and let it set in.

Okay, I'm clear. For Zach, and for all of us who suffer from any form of physical pain, here's a new perspective . . .

THE MIND-BODY CONNECTION

Think for a moment about any chronic pain or physical conditions that show up in your own life. Do you have back or neck pain? Do you struggle with your gut? Are you dealing with any chronic autoimmune condition? Do you have skin issues? Now take a moment to consider what's happening in your life when these conditions flare up. Are you stressed at work when your back goes out? Does your stomach go into knots when you feel anxious about something you cannot control? Are you enduring emotional distress when your autoimmune condition flares up? Take a moment to reflect on the situational and emotional patterns that unfold when you experience these physical issues.

Do you notice any common themes around what's happening when you experience these conditions? Is it possible that stress is a contributor? Could it be that your body is responding to an emotional disturbance? Is it possible that your physical condition is a response to pent-up anger or rage?

If you're someone who's struggled with chronic pain or an ongoing physical condition, the mere concept that there could be a psychological component to your pain might really make you mad. Particularly in Western cultures, as we've grown to rely on an allopathic approach to healing, the idea that physical conditions could be protecting against emotional disturbances can be hard to grasp. When someone is in the midst of a physical crisis, it can even seem inconsiderate for you to imply that the pain comes from impermissible feelings. Nevertheless, when we are stuck in chronic pain, we're often willing to do whatever it takes to experience relief. So ride the wave of that willingness now and keep an open mind. Stay curious about what lies beneath the pain. And stay open to the idea that Self can help address what's ailing you in your physical body: there's evidence for IFS-inspired treatments not only relieving the subjective experience of stress, but measurably lowering blood levels of the stress hormone cortisol.[1]

I know all too well how physical pain and conditions are all-consuming, taking up your time and distracting you from living a joyful life. But *distracting* is the operative word. From an IFS perspective, the Protector's role is to distract you from the exiled emotions (repressed trauma, anger, fear, shame, and so on). As long as we're distracted, we don't have to focus on the root-cause condition: inner psychological pain.

I'm in no way suggesting that your physical pain or suffering isn't happening—I'm just suggesting you look more deeply at what's underneath it. There's a physiological response to repressed emotions, and it's called stress. When you're emotionally triggered by an exiled feeling, your nervous system goes into a stress response: fight, flight, or freeze. This stress response will silently send your body into a dysregulated state that can ignite a myriad of physical issues like back pain, gastrological issues, and so on. The stress response creates inflammation, tension, and a slowing down of the digestive system. In this stressful state, one is indeed experiencing physical symptoms that may require medical attention. Often the medical diagnosis will offer a pill, a shot, or even a surgery to put out the fire of the pain. But that fire may only be extinguished temporarily, if at all. The modern approach to pain and conditions stems from the question: "How can we fix this?" But what if instead you considered contemplating, "What's emotionally behind this?"

Again, I'm not trying to minimize your pain, question your diagnosis, or suggest that you not listen to your doctor.

You are indeed having a physical issue, after all. But let me ask you this: "How's that approach been going for you?" If your response is anything other than "Amazing," consider this: instead of just trying to fix your physical conditions, you could choose to check in with them. Perhaps you could take the pressure off your body by becoming curious about the underlying emotional disturbances that may be triggering it. When you acknowledge the protective role the body plays, you open your consciousness to a psychological Self-led path to relief that addresses the underlying condition—exiled emotional distress.

CONSIDER THE BODY AS A PROTECTOR

Throughout my therapeutic journey, I've been supported by the teachings of Dr. John Sarno, the renowned author of *Healing Back Pain: The Mind-Body Connection* and the creator of TMS (tension myoneural syndrome or mind-body syndrome). The thesis of Dr. Sarno's work is that the underlying cause of pain is the mind's defense mechanisms against impermissible emotions such as rage, anxiety, and fear. The idea is that physical pain and chronic conditions suppress unwanted emotions in the unconscious. When attention is directed toward the pain, it deflects focus, thereby suppressing the exiled emotions.

According to Dr. Sarno, in an effort to shut down these unconscious thoughts, the brain focuses conscious pain onto a physical symptom, such as back pain, neck pain, jaw tension, and even other symptoms such as gastrointestinal issues, autoimmune disorders, etc. In what he termed *distraction syndrome*, the brain is focused on the pain, which works to protect against extreme psychological disturbances by acting as a distraction. If the brain is focused on the pain, blood flow is cut off, stress is induced, inflammation is increased, and the body responds with more tension. Over time the pain or condition worsens. When we are suffering with physical pain or an undesirable physical condition, there's only one focus: the painful condition. Whether we realize it or not, it can often feel safer to suffer from physical pain than be faced with the exiled emotions underneath it.

Pain is often a frontline response when vulnerable Exiles are triggered, working as a defense mechanism against perceived threats or harm. From an IFS perspective, by approaching body pain with empathy, curiosity, and mindfulness, you can uncover the protective intentions behind the pain. You can engage in a healing dialogue with these parts and transform your relationship with pain by addressing underlying emotional distress. If you offer curiosity and compassionate connection to your physical Protector parts, then you help soften the edges.

Dr. Sarno emphasized not ignoring physical symptoms, advising patients to stay on medication and adhere to doctors' protocols while embracing a new perspective. I share the same sentiment. While I firmly believe in the psychosomatic effects on the body and recognize these aspects as Protectors, I also place my trust in medical professionals and benefit from their support. It's crucial to emphasize that the approach we are discussing in this chapter is not intended to replace a traditional medical approach but rather to complement and support it. Both perspectives can work harmoniously to enhance overall well-being.

In my case, my repressed trauma caused me to have severe gastrointestinal issues. In acute moments of physical distress, I had to rely on doctors to help me. The medical approach to healing offered me temporary relief and put out the fire. However, it wasn't the solution to the underlying problem. Healing the repressed emotions was.

The time in my life when my gastro issues were the absolute worst was the exact time when I remembered repressed sexual trauma from my childhood. In the months leading up to the memory, my stomach was an absolute mess and I was diagnosed with gastritis. It was like the stomach acid was eating away at my stomach lining the same way the memory was eating away at my psyche. When I did finally remember, I was confronted directly with the Exile that I'd been trying to protect for so long. I was terrified of the feelings I was facing, and my stomach flared more than ever. I couldn't eat without extreme pain, and I suffered from heartburn to the point where I lost my voice from the reflux. My stomach took up the majority of my attention. It was all I could focus on. Why? Because it was protecting me from focusing on the exiled emotions that had surfaced. My stomach pain was distracting me from the most horrific emotional pain. The fire in my belly was an extreme distraction from my repressed exiled parts.

Through my inner inquiry, I came to see how my stomach symptoms show up in response to stress, fear, or any time I was triggered. Whenever I'd get flooded with a PTSD response, my stomach would go into knots. Then all my attention would be focused on the stomach pain. Obsessing over my stomach redirected my focus off the triggered Exile and onto my body. My stomach was a Protector.

While my stomach conditions were working hard to distract me from the resurfaced memories, the pain was also destroying me. Ultimately I had to find a long-term solution to the chronic condition. That's when I surrendered fully to healing my body by healing the trauma. By dedicating myself to the healing journey of my inner exiled parts, I shifted my attention away from my physical body to confront and address my suppressed emotions—the root cause of the stress. This radical redirect offered me the path to relief.

AWARENESS IS THE FIRST STEP

I have another Protector part that's been around for as long as I can remember. This part goes into overdrive, clenching tightly to keep everything intact—which manifests as chronic jaw tension. For decades, this jaw tension has worked around the clock, clenching all day and all throughout the night. It has broken my teeth, caused TMJ, and even affected my vocal health. Eventually the symptoms became so severe that I could no longer ignore them. I had to become curious about what lived beneath the incessant clenching—opening my heart to know more.

Through the support of IFS, I came to accept that it wasn't just a physical symptom, but instead *a Protector part.* The jaw tension is always in the background, silently holding on—protecting.

Seeking relief, I finally chose to offer my jaw some attention—I chose to stop ignoring it and check in instead. I got curious about it: *it's tight; it's breaking teeth; it feels desperate; clenching; painful; it's sad.* I leaned in to the sadness. *What else do I know about that sadness? It believes that if it's not clenching, it's not safe.* Becoming even more curious, I heard the jaw tension speak out: *I'm terrified, I'm young, and I am scared. I'm fucking terrified. I don't want to let go.* Then I asked the tense jaw part, "What do you need?" *I need to protect myself!*

In my first conversation with the jaw tension, I was blended with the part, but I still noticed that a touch of Self energy came through—I felt a slight sensation of relief. By merely focusing my attention on the physical symptom and seeing it as a Protector, I could allow space for it to soften. For the first time, I was able to listen to my jaw tension as a Protector and hear why it was working so hard. Instead of labeling it a physical symptom, I chose to witness it as a part. Instead of ignoring it or pushing past it, I was able to be with it.

I could perceive this part as a young girl desperately striving to maintain a sense of safety. She didn't believe there was any other way. I created a supportive space for her to share her sadness, even allowing tears to flow.

My choice and courage to witness the jaw tension as a Protector provided me with a fresh and clear perspective, along with a subtle sense of relief. A little relief was enough to begin the journey of letting Self help. The goal of this process wasn't to force the jaw Protector out of its role, but rather to begin to accept that the physical tension was a psychosomatic response to repressed sadness, fear, and even anger. The jaw tension was not a symptom, it was a Protector. This revelation offered me the Self energy of compassion and clarity, and I recognized how hard my jaw has worked to keep me safe.

I LET THE PAIN SPEAK

Throughout the 2020 COVID-19 pandemic, as the case was for many people, my Exiles and Protectors were activated. In particular, my jaw was clenching more than ever. I knew the stress of that time was causing increased physical tension, so I committed to listening to the emotions behind the tension. For a year I diligently used my journaling to unearth the anger and emotions concealed beneath the pain. I called this journaling practice "rage on the page." I'd listen to binaural music that would open up my brain's bilateral functioning and, in effect, help me process big emotions just through writing. I'd journal my rage onto the page for 20 minutes. Then I'd follow the journaling with a 20-minute meditation while listening to the binaural music. My commitment to this practice gave me relief. Spending time with the jaw tension every day allowed me to create space for it to be heard. I gave myself full permission to let it all out in an unfiltered way. I'd unleash my emotions onto the page, allowing the subconscious fears, rage, and anxiety to surface and be heard—Self was there to receive it. This year-long process was a profound opportunity to let my physical jaw pain speak, release, and reprocess.

To genuinely heal this protective part, it's imperative to cultivate trust between the part and Self. Although the part feels secure expressing itself during daily rage-on-the-page sessions, there's a lingering doubt about fully trusting that it's safe to let it all go. Even as I write this chapter, the awareness of my jaw pain persists. I can sense into the sadness and rage beneath it, accompanied by an inclination to suppress these emotions. Old shame and terror echo underneath the jaw tension. The only solution is to let Self help.

It's important for me to truthfully share that while I've experienced great relief in my stomach and other physical conditions, my jaw tension is far from gone. It is still playing a protective role in my internal system. In fact, the more I let Self help, the more the jaw tension tries to protect against it. The jaw is a silent Protector that works in the background with one eye open all the time, anticipating potential threats. I identify this jaw tension as my last frontier. I can see clearly that this jaw tension is a Protector part, and I can honor that it's holding on to something that's not yet ready to be revealed—a physical reminder that there is more to be healed and that there's more trust in Self to be established.

Embracing my jaw tension as a guiding force provides me with the opportunity to check in with it daily rather than dismiss it. Even as I write this chapter, I am deliberately tuning in to my jaw, discerning the tension and the underlying grief it holds.

Grief is the word it repeats to me when I check in. Grief: an impermissible emotion that is so hard to face that my jaw literally locks it up. In this moment, as I write about the jaw tension, I'm checking in with it, and I feel profound compassion for my young part. It's worked so hard to keep me safe from the terror, the rage, and the unimaginable grief. The grief of feeling unlovable, uncared for, or inadequate. The grief stemming from the loss of my childhood innocence. The grief of confronting the harsh truths of my past. As I articulate this grief, I sense my jaw easing its grip. A subtle tremor courses through my body, and every muscle in my face settles. Self is emerging.

I didn't expect this relief, but just writing this part of the chapter gave voice to grief, allowing Self energy to come forward. I didn't even know that grief was the emotion underneath it until now. Writing has offered the part the freedom to come into my conscious awareness and reveal why it's been working so hard. It's been covering up the unspeakable grief of my past.

This connection to Self came as a gift to me. I didn't have a plan for this truth to be revealed; I just cleared space for my jaw tension to be recognized. As I compassionately connected to my jaw tension through writing, it was able to let out what it's been working so hard to hold in. The creative process of writing cleared space for that clarity and compassion to come through. My writing revealed what my body was holding on to.

Now it's your turn.

WRITING WITH YOUR BODY PARTS

I've found that writing freely onto the page can be a profound portal for parts to share truth and for Self to set in. Building upon the writing practices in Chapter 4, I'm going to encourage you to use your journal as your guide to Self energy. If you're open to connecting with a physical Protector that has been a source of pain and suffering, follow the guidance provided here. However, if considering your physical symptoms as psychosomatic conditions feels triggering or overwhelming for any reason, trust that feeling and come back to this at another time.

This exercise is a dialogue with the Protector parts associated with body pain. Through gentle exploration and guided self-inquiry, you can uncover the underlying emotions, beliefs, or memories that these parts are trying to protect you from facing. It is essential to approach these Protector parts with openness, patience, and respect, allowing them to express themselves fully.

Follow my guidance and check in with your body to cultivate a compassionate and curious attitude toward whatever pain may be present—when you give it space to speak, your body has a lot to reveal. Rather than viewing your body as the enemy or as a physical symptom that has to be healed or overcome, you can practice approaching your physical pain or condition with empathy by acknowledging its presence and seeking to understand its purpose.

Start by contemplating any form of persistent physical pain or inflammatory condition that may be chronic or may arise at specific times in your life. If it feels safe, **choose to check in with it.**

Now become curious, offering this physical pain your attention and presence. Ask the part:

- How long have you been around?
- Are there any other feelings or sensations you want to reveal?
- Do you have any thoughts you want to share?
- Is there an image or a story that needs to come forward?

Become even more curious, offering the part space to come forward.

What else do you want to know?

Continue opening up space for more curiosity until you feel a connection to the part.

Next, check in more by asking the part what it needs from you (Self). Encourage the part to freely express itself on the page. Let it all out. This is a chance to unleash your emotions on paper, allowing for the release of any pent-up feelings. Open your journal and write until you experience a sense of relief.

When your writing feels complete, close your eyes and breathe with the part. Allow the presence of Self to come through naturally. Trust in your connection, and know that in this open state you have clear access to Self energy. If you feel any C qualities come forward, breathe into them and sense into the Self energy that's coming through these feelings. Allow this Self energy to magnify by following the guided meditation below. To listen to the guided audio of this practice, go to DearGabby.com/SelfHelpResources.

Note: As you engage in this meditation, be mindful of your breathing. With each inhale, expand your diaphragm, and on each exhale, allow your diaphragm to relax. This breathing technique ensures your breaths aren't shallow, providing you with relief.

Breathe into the sensations in your body that may still feel tense or painful or unpleasant.

Breathe out.

Breathe in and notice the sensations, and offer them your breath.

Breathe out with an energy of acceptance.

Breathe into the body part, allowing it to be present with the tension.

Breathe out.

As you breathe in and out, visualize calm energy surrounding the pain.

Invite the body part to settle with your breath.

Breathe in and feel into the sensations in your body.

Breathe out.

Let any visions or images come to mind. Remain willing to receive a calm connection.

Breathe in and notice any calmness setting in.

Breathe out more acceptance and a sigh of relief.

Breathe in any newfound clarity.

Breathe out.

Breathe in any sensations of curiosity.

Breathe out.

Breathe in the feeling of connection.

Breathe out.

Breathe in, offering up compassion.

Breathe out.

Breathe in any sensations of creativity.

Breathe out.

Breathe into the openhearted space of confidence.

Breathe out.

Breathe in a deep sense of confidence.

Breathe out.

Notice any of the C qualities that are present in your system.

Give the feelings breath.

Take some time to sit with the qualities of Self that have come through.

Relish any connection to Self energy.

Let Self multiply.

My hope is that this practice offers you a whole new perception of your physical body and pain. By merely noticing that pain emerges from a protective intention, you can develop a more compassionate relationship with your body. Check in a bit more and reflect on the process:

- Can you sense a compassionate presence toward the pain?
- Are you able to observe the pain without judgment, bringing awareness to the sensations and emotions that arise?

- Are you able to sense into Self?
- Did this practice help you release any feelings of hopelessness?

Notice what it feels like inside your body now.

This process of connecting to your body Protectors offers the Protector part awareness, acceptance, and an opening for Self. As you build up understanding and compassion, you'll be able to begin the journey of addressing the root causes of your pain. The need for protection diminishes, and physical symptoms reduce or disappear. If you have a spontaneous experience of relief from pain, do your best not to judge it. Other Protectors will want to shut it down and return to a diagnosis or a reason that it wouldn't go away. Be mindful of the resistance that comes through, and gently ask those resistant parts to step aside. Give yourself as much time as you can to take in the full body acceptance that it is indeed possible. If you really commit to the relief, it has the power to take over and be your new normal.

When you clear space for your body parts to speak, they can release. When you breathe into that released state, Self can make physical adjustments. Freedom and empowerment lie in our experience of this relief. When you experience this shift once, you'll no longer feel powerless over your pain, and instead you'll know that with release comes great relief.

Now that you have had the chance to witness your physical pain as a Protector, you may feel some relief. It's also possible that you may have noticed another Protector step in front of the pain to block you from revealing deeper emotions. No matter the outcome, trust that this is a process. The next time you notice physical pain or symptoms arise, instead of pushing against it, stressing about it, or trying to numb it, check in. Give your body the chance to speak up and reveal whatever it is that you need to know. Creating space for your body parts to speak gives them the freedom to be seen and offer you real insights. You don't have to try to figure everything out; instead, ask the part.

A devotional curiosity and willingness to check in are the greatest Self-help tools in your toolbox. Instead of overriding your physical body, you can tune in and ask it what it needs. Your body can become your guide to knowing more of what your inner world wants to reveal.

OPEN YOUR HEART TO THE MIRACLE

At my latest physical exam, I experienced a miracle moment. I sat across from my doctor and shared how I was feeling. "My jaw is still acting up, which is my sign that there's deeper emotional healing coming through. My gut is doing great as I feel a strong sense of safety and resilience inside. I feel empowered, and I honor my body as a guide."

My doctor looked at me with a huge smile and said, "Wow, I wish that all my patients could have that much compassion and connection toward their bodies."

The foundational principles of IFS and the check-in process offer you the chance to establish a compassionate connection to your physical Protectors. The process of acknowledging and engaging with physical pain as a Protector will help you open up to transformative shifts inside and out. You no longer have to feel like the victim of your physical pain, but instead, you have a new way to perceive it.

THE INNER HEALER

I shared this chapter with my husband, Zach, slightly anxious about drawing attention to his lingering back issues that I mentioned at the start of the chapter. Yet I truly believed that even a spark of curiosity would ignite Self to lead him toward understanding and relief. And I was right. As he absorbed the content, a seed of awareness was planted. From that point on, whenever Zach became aware of his pain, he made a conscious choice not to dwell solely on the physical sensation. Instead, he used the check-in process to explore how he was feeling at that moment. Every instance of pain became an opportunity for connection—to identify any emotional stress or pain that might be lurking beneath the surface. Remarkably, within just a few minutes of this practice, Zach often finds significant relief.

That same relief is available to you now. This practice has the power to open you up to a Self-guided path to physical peace. Let Self help your body develop a more harmonious relationship with your pain, leading to increased well-being, emotional resilience, and a sense of wholeness. My prayer is that this new perception offers you relief through just knowing that you always have a wise healer inside.

CHAPTER 9

FIREFIGHTERS

Last year I was interviewed on a podcast hosted by a vibrant 28-year-old woman. Sitting beside me, dressed in low-rise jeans and a T-shirt that showcased her toned stomach, she excitedly started the conversation. Meanwhile, I struggled to maintain my composure. The studio lights were blinding me and her assistant, just off to the side, was pounding away on her keyboard—click-click-click. But as soon as the host started talking about her struggles with food addiction, unresolved PTSD, and anxiety, we found a connection. Our eyes met, and in that moment compassion flooded in. The lights and the noise disappeared and all I saw was a reflection of myself in her. It was like looking at my younger self and all her fearful parts sitting right in front of me. Afraid to let go of control, driven by relentless anxiety, and eagerly seeking solutions.

"Gabby, how are you so at peace today?" the host asked with genuine curiosity.

"I'm at peace because today I love every part of who I am."

She seemed blown away by this response and continued to ask questions, desperately seeking answers to her unresolved addictive patterns. For the next 40 minutes, I was transported back, sitting with my 25-year-old self, offering her the guidance I wish I had received at that pivotal time in my life.

In this openhearted conversation, I was able to help the host see that her food addiction was not a problem with her but instead a Protector part of her—a Firefighter trying to put out the flames of impermissible feelings from her childhood. Since she had alluded to childhood trauma and unresolved stress, I thought it was possible that her past overeating was the way she'd maintained control over her exiled emotions. Our conversation offered her the chance to witness her addiction through a new lens—the lens of compassion. I guided her to see how hard this addicted Firefighter worked to keep her from facing her past.

She also opened up about grappling with workaholism and compulsive exercise. I guided her to recognize that these behaviors were other types of Protectors, working hard to keep the younger traumatized parts at bay. These Protectors were "socially acceptable" and often praised—but they were extreme Firefighters nonetheless.

As the conversation wrapped up, I noticed that for a moment she was able to release some attachment to her parts and view their intense patterns with a touch of compassion. While this one conversation wasn't the antidote to her decades of suffering, it was a moment of clarity ignited by the Self energy within her. This clarity offered her a new perspective on her addiction—a compassionate understanding that she couldn't have contemplated before. This new perspective offered her a glimmer of Self that was enough to spark a shift inside.

That same clarity is what I hope to offer you now. I want to help you witness your more extreme and addictive

Protector parts in a new light—to understand them for what they really are: Firefighters.

FIREFIGHTERS

Firefighters are our most impulsive protective parts, leaping into action when our emotional flames become too overwhelming. Firefighters show up when our Managers can no longer hold it together. When the trigger is so intense that we have to go to extreme measures to numb the painful feelings. Firefighters often manifest as extreme or addictive behaviors, including bingeing, alcoholism, codependent attachments, gambling, rage, and even suicidal ideation.

Firefighters have unique and effective ways of turning off the valve of our impermissible emotions to anesthetize the pain. They are excellent distractors, ready to step in when all else fails and do whatever it takes to put out the fire of the Exiles.

It's possible to become deeply intertwined with and dependent on our internal Firefighter's protection mechanisms, to the point where we believe they are our only source of safety from the overwhelming emotions we've hidden for so long. When overtaken by a Firefighter, Self energy is masked under the weight of our yearning to escape our Exiles. And while it's crucial to remember that the power of choice never truly leaves us, in these moments Self becomes overshadowed by our Protectors.

These parts can be destructive and all-consuming, and my hope is to guide you to see them differently and to understand their motivations. Firefighters act out from a place of protection—their intention is to shield us from the forbidden pain of our past. When we open our heart and mind to witness our Firefighters through the lens of Self, we can develop a nurturing perspective on our Firefighter parts. Instead of blaming and shaming our Firefighters, we can open our hearts to them, allowing Self to come through. This approach unveils a powerful path to self-acceptance and long-term healing.

In this chapter we're going to gently witness your more extreme, addictive, or dissociative Protectors—your Firefighters. We'll strip away the complexity of these extreme parts and see them through the simplicity of their core desire: the incessant need to feel safe. This is a process of witnessing through the lens of love—through the lens of Self. A perceptual shift that can guide you toward deeper healing.

A NEW PERSPECTIVE

The intention of this chapter is to guide you to witness the genuine protective intentions of Firefighters: to protect you from exiled wounds that you're not ready to face. For example, one of my extreme Firefighters is dissociation—my ability to totally check out from the world, go numb, and leave my body. Dissociation, my longtime Firefighter, has stood by me for as long as I can remember. When I was a child, this part helped me numb out when the reality of my unsafe circumstances became too overwhelming. There were moments in therapy when dissociation would literally put me to sleep in order to shut down an exiled part that wasn't ready to surface. I can clearly recognize the invaluable assistance this Firefighter has provided during times of trauma and heightened stress.

Dissociation was such a strong Protector that it actually shielded a repressed trauma memory from my consciousness for over three decades. As I've noted, it wasn't until I was 36 and 10 years sober that I recalled a particular traumatic event from my childhood. The emergence of this memory was as revealing as it was unsettling, as I had spent 30 years not knowing the reason for my suffering, addiction, anxiety, and pain. The dissociative part of me had buried this memory deep within my subconscious, all the while seeking external mechanisms (such as addiction, control, and anxiety) to keep the traumatized parts of myself in exile. When I brought this up with my therapist, she suggested that the memory emerged because I was "safe enough to remember." By then, with 10 years of sobriety and extensive personal development work, including IFS therapy, I had built a strong foundation. The inner safety I had developed allowed my subconscious exiled parts to be revealed through a dream.

This was the one of scariest experiences of my life as it sent me back into the extreme feelings of my Exile. After this revelation I stayed close to home and avoided social interaction. I became engrossed in Netflix and over a two-month span, I watched every single season of *Scandal.* Unbeknownst to me, the show, and particularly the star character, Olivia Pope—a confident and courageous woman—not only instilled hope in me but also provided a means of numbing the overwhelming pain of that period. The addictive nature of binge-watching *Scandal* was a form of protection. It gave me a way to numb out.

FIREFIGHTERS IN DISGUISE

Firefighters have different risk levels. There are low-risk Firefighter patterns involving everyday activities like social media, screen time, overeating sugar, gaming, sports, exercise, gossip, sleep, flirting, and shopping. In my case of binge-watching *Scandal,* using the show as a form of dissociation was far less risky than picking up a drink to numb the pain and sabotaging a decade of sobriety. But I still consider this a Firefighter pattern because I excessively watched the show to put out the fire of overwhelming emotions. Higher-risk Firefighters include drug abuse, alcoholism, sex addiction, gambling, overspending, disordered eating, emotional eating, self-harm, suicidal thoughts, and violence. Whatever the level of extremity, the intention remains: anesthetize the unbearable exiled feelings and put out the fire.

There are also socially acceptable Firefighters that can be harder to identify, including extreme people-pleasing, work addiction, or overachieving. One socially acceptable Firefighter that ran my world for many years was the workaholic part. This part developed when, upon getting sober, I quickly transferred my drug addiction into a new addiction to work. (Workaholism is a particularly common addictive strategy for Firefighters when there isn't a strong connection to Self.[1])

While my dedication to my work brought immense joy and helped many people, it also became an excessive means for me to numb out my exiled, dissociated childhood trauma. As my complete lack of work/life balance started to spiral out of control, my physical well-being deteriorated, and I experienced debilitating nervous breakdowns, I finally accepted that this seemingly commendable "work ethic" was in fact an addictive pattern. It took years for me to come to this realization—after all, I was praised for my successes and how much I could accomplish.

It's important to call this out because often Firefighters that are deemed socially acceptable can be hard to identify. For instance, a parent may write off their kid's incessant screen time as "Oh, she's just a teenager," thereby overriding her underlying depression. Or maybe you're praised for how much you show up for others at the expense of your own well-being. You don't have to be an addict to have overpowering Firefighters on high alert at all times.

TAKE IT SLOW

Be mindful that if even witnessing these parts feels overwhelming, you can just read through the chapter and not apply the practices. If at any point you feel overwhelmed or activated by this chapter, please consider seeking IFS therapeutic support; see the resources page at DearGabby.com/SelfHelpResources. It's important not to lift the veil on a part that is not yet ready to be seen.

While my hope is to guide you toward a compassionate awareness of your Firefighters, I recognize that it may be triggering at first. You may continue to perceive addiction and destructive behavior as something you can't accept, let alone extend compassion toward. I understand if you're having that resistance, and I suggest you don't push yourself into this perspective. All I recommend is that you remain willing to learn more about Firefighters and their core intentions. The path to healing Firefighters' extreme patterns doesn't come through judgment or force but through compassionate connection. Understanding the why behind their motivations will offer you the possibility of compassion rather than control.

Firefighters commonly manifest as addictive parts that can be very defensive. These extreme and often addicted parts have been judged and shamed by parts of you and the world around you. Firefighters are deeply intertwined with their protective roles, making it challenging for them to connect with Self. These parts live with the belief "I must maintain control over the Exiles," doing whatever is necessary to put out the flames of any activated emotions. The parts feel ashamed of their actions, often berating themselves as well as facing criticism from the outside world. Consider, for instance, an alcoholic part that continually falls into the same addictive pattern, or an extremely codependent part that sacrifices its own well-being for the sake of an unhealthy relationship. These parts are often shamed by the outside world for their destructiveness and blamed internally by other judgmental Protectors. This keeps the parts in a shame-and-blame loop.

I personally understand the shame that can shadow these extreme, addicted Firefighters. In my early 20s, before I got sober, I was severely addicted to romantic relationships. I'd leap from one relationship to another, grasping at an outside sense of safety that I could not find within. The dread of being single equaled the fear of death—and I don't say that lightly. My codependent Firefighter part was so extreme and petrified of being alone that she'd sacrifice her own well-being and happiness just to cling to a relationship.

It was around that time that my oldest friend confronted me about my codependency, saying, "You can never just be on your own, Gab. You've been like this since high school." His words filled me with shame, and that day I made a vow to no longer need a relationship. I put down the boyfriend, only to instantly pick up cocaine. In an attempt to escape the shame of codependency, I fell into another addiction, which in the end would bring even more shame.

Initially you may think you have control over your habits, but as more addictions or destructive behaviors accumulate, they can lead to serious consequences and even thoughts of self-harm. The hope of practicing Self-help is that you can address each addictive Firefighter as a unique part, offering it curiosity, connection, and compassion. Instead of covering up your Firefighters with other addictive behaviors, you can consciously support them—help them from sinking. Each time you choose to check in and connect to a Firefighter, it offers a chance to feel genuinely supported and guided on a long-lasting path to recovery.

I've spent hours of my life listening to the stories of fellow addicts in recovery. While each is unique, we share a common bond: the experience of grief and trauma. I firmly believe that trauma is the underlying cause of Firefighters' extreme, reactive behaviors. Every addict I've come across has, in some form, confronted profound childhood experiences that overwhelmed their ability to cope, resulting in the development of Managers and, eventually, extreme and addictive Firefighters.

In an interview on my *Dear Gabby* podcast, Dr. Gabor Maté, the world-renowned trauma expert and best-selling author, said, "Trauma is not what happens to you. Trauma is what happens inside you as a result of what happened to you." The internal rupture of safety and innocence is what propels trauma and what keeps it stuck. The sad truth is that Firefighters and Managers have such a bad rap. We've judged them and blamed them for so much of our suffering when all the while they were hard at work trying to minimize it.

FIREFIGHTERS CANNOT BE FORCED TO CHANGE

Writing about Firefighters is surprisingly emotional for me. There's a dance between the simplicity of making a choice to heal and the fear of letting go of what seems to be the most effective form of protection. Letting go of a Firefighter can feel like losing a best friend. We grow to rely on these parts to show up for us, and we become so blended with them that we fear that we can't live without them.

Often when we contemplate facing a Firefighter, controlling parts emerge to try to convince us that to change an addictive Firefighter pattern we must follow a rigid set of rules and rally against our cravings or reactivity. The fear of slipping back into familiar yet destructive and addictive patterns can be paralyzing. Attempting to force the part to stop isn't a path to recovery, it's just another Protector trying to keep your internal system under control.

When Firefighters are shamed or forced to stop their addictive patterns, they often move into denial. An example looks like this: "He's been better lately, less aggressive—he's really trying," says my close friend Ali about her husband. For more than two years, Ali has confided in me about her husband's struggle with alcohol abuse, which sometimes escalates into alarming and aggressive behavior. She explains that whenever she tries to control his behavior or force him to stop, he shows up with conflicting parts—the defensive part that insists, "It's just a few beers" and the remorseful part that pledges, "I'll never drink again, I promise." A few weeks will go by and I'll get a hopeful text from Ali trying to prove to me (and herself) that things are getting better. But I always get a text a few days later that he's relapsed.

Trying to control a Firefighter to get it to stop only makes things worse. Remember that most people don't want to harm themselves or others. No one *wants* to destroy their life with addictive and extreme patterns. But the more rigid and shaming we are toward our Firefighters, the more shame they feel and the more activated they become. Internal shame and a coercive demeanor only serve to keep

Firefighters stuck in their extreme and destructive patterns. No amount of shame, force, or blame will help a Firefighter.

Take a moment to reflect on the most extreme parts of you. Maybe you've spent your life burdened by disordered eating as a way of trying to stay in control of your Exiles. Maybe you have a work addiction—you work so you don't have to feel. Or maybe you suffer from addiction to substances. As you witness these parts, consider now how you feel about them. Do you hate them? Do you try to shut them down? If so, how's that working out?

The path to truly healing addiction isn't paved with rigid perfection or force, but with a series of choices that shape your daily experience. Consider the wisdom of the 12 Steps and the concept of "one day at a time." What if, instead of fixating on the complexity of the journey, you focused on the simple act of choosing to check in one day at a time? Or one minute at a time?

FREEDOM FROM ADDICTION COMES FROM CHOICE

Take a moment to suspend any disbelief and imagine this: You can begin each day by checking with the parts that are present—opening the door for Self to set in. As the day unfolds, you encounter the inevitable triggers and frustrations that life presents. It's in these moments that the power of choice truly shines. You have the ability to pause, take a breath, and opt to check in. You're no longer at the mercy of your triggers; you're equipped with a choice that empowers you to tend to your activated part and help it settle. Then, an hour after your morning intention, you're triggered by a situation that once would have sent you spiraling. Instead of succumbing to the activation, you pause and check in with the part. In that pause, presence emerges. You feel the feelings and sensations that arise, and you exercise choice—you consciously decide your next action. You're not concerned about perfection. Instead you're focused on consistently remembering to exercise your freedom to choose again.

How does it feel to contemplate living in this way? I recognize that this can seem impossible if you're stuck in an addictive Firefighter pattern. However, I invite you to consider a new possibility: that when it comes to our extreme patterns, we do indeed have the power to choose to seek Self for help. On October 2, 2005, I made a choice to get sober and seek help. For the past 19 years I have continued to wake up and humbly reinforce that choice. This long-term recovery is filled with freedom and ease because I've chosen one day at a time to let Self enter in and show me that path toward deep inner healing. While in this moment choice may feel far from your reach, consider my story as a powerful example of what's possible for you.

WHEN FACED WITH WHAT SEEMS LIKE AN IMPOSSIBLE CHOICE

I once delivered a talk on the transformative power of choice and our ability to redirect our lives in an instant. On that day my inner motivational speaker part came to life, coexisting with a strong connection to Self energy. The blend of positive motivation and genuine Self energy flooded the auditorium.

Throughout the presentation, I confidently emphasized that in any given moment we possess the choice to turn inward or, alternatively, veer off into fear and be taken over by our Protectors. When we choose to turn inward, embrace curiosity, and foster connections, we have the power to redirect our lives.

I sensed the audience fluctuating between belief and skepticism, which gave me the opportunity to engage with the skeptics during the Q and A session. Guiding them through the check-in process, I helped them experience the power of choice firsthand as they redirected their focus and opened up to Self-guided decisions. This real-time transformation allowed the audience to grasp the profound impact even a subtle shift in choice can have.

As the talk concluded, I sat on the edge of the stage, meeting attendees. In the queue I noticed a burly man fixated on me. He was next in line, and although I felt safe, I couldn't ignore his intense energy—a mix of anger and aggression emanating from him.

When it was his turn, he approached with a powerful defensive energy. "You say we have a choice, but I don't have a damn choice in how I feel! I struggle with mental illness and addiction; I can't just choose to shift out of that."

I took a deep breath and centered myself. Gazing into his eyes as if we were alone in the room, I replied, "You are absolutely right. When we have mental illness and severe addiction, choice can seem unattainable." I went on to share my own battle with suicidal depression and how, in the end, my only choice was to surrender and seek psychiatric support. Thankfully I had enough access to Self in that moment to allow a genuine compassionate connection to set in. I saw myself in him—my addiction, my mental illness, my sense of helplessness. I felt connected to him, I was calm in my body and my heart was open. I was in Self energy.

"Can I give you a hug?" I asked. He agreed without hesitation. I wrapped my arms around his broad chest, holding him with genuine love and compassion. His energy softened, and his rage melted away as tears streamed down his face. In this embrace he could feel fully seen and supported by the open heart of Self energy.

In those moments I didn't need words, my experiences, or my stories. All that was required, for both of us, was the presence of Self.

When I released the hug, I kept my hands on his shoulders, looking directly into his eyes. The man who had appeared threatening moments ago now resembled an innocent child, his eyes wide with tears. "Thank you. I wasn't expecting that," he said.

"Thank you for choosing to open your heart," I replied.

GET INTO RELATIONSHIP RATHER THAN CONTROL

As Gabor Maté says, "Instead of asking why the addiction, ask why the pain?" In my experience when an IFS therapist works with a Firefighter part, instead of asking, "Why do you keep doing this?" they'll ask, "How is this part trying to help you?" Addicted Firefighters should not be asked to provide an excuse but be given the chance to share their reason.

My IFS teacher Cece Sykes, LCSW, author of *Internal Family Systems Therapy for Addictions*, breaks it down like this: when one is in an addiction cycle, the Managers and Firefighters are going after one another. Sykes calls this the "addictive processes battle." IFS teaches that the internal experience of an addict is described through three distinct parts at odds with one another:

- The Blame/Manager part that perpetuates self-criticism, insisting that the addict is out of control and will never change.

- The Flame/Firefighter part that expresses a defiant attitude, believing they deserve their addiction and resisting any attempts at intervention.
- The Shame/Exile part that instills a deep sense of hopelessness and isolation, as if there is something fundamentally wrong with them and change is impossible due to past failed efforts to control their addiction.

These three unique parts are at war with one another, keeping one stuck in the addictive cycle of blame, flame, and shame.

What I find most supportive about the IFS approach to addiction and Firefighters is the emphasis on how to relate to your Firefighters' extreme and addictive patterns. The IFS approach is focused on compassionately connecting to the Firefighters and getting into a relationship with them rather than attempting to control them.

Rather than attempting to control the Firefighters' addictive parts, IFS advocates for a compassionate and curious approach to establishing a relationship with them by asking them to open up and share their experience. Through the check-in process, you can become curious about the story behind the addiction, and the Firefighter feels more connected, clearing space for Self to come through.

You can establish a relationship by offering addictive parts messages of connection rather than control. By checking in with the part rather than trying to control it, you offer up an opportunity for connection. Instead of shunning the part, you're offering it a message like *I just want to get to know you.* Any form of connection helps Firefighters feel seen and respected—recognized in their innocence.

Remember, extreme Firefighter parts are desperately trying to keep you safe. If even for a moment you could shift your perception of your Firefighters and experience a glimmer of Self, you'd offer them a miracle: the chance to be seen in their innocence.

Contemplating this will likely activate a Manager part. Maybe it feels scary to even consider letting a Firefighter off the hook. I get it, this might take time. But by opening your heart to perceive your Firefighters in this way, you can expand the possibilities for relationship rather than control.

An inner paradigm shift occurs when we offer up this Self-led query to our Firefighters. Instead of judgment, we choose compassion.

SAFELY CHECKING IN WITH A FIREFIGHTER

Your Firefighters are not alone in their addictive and unconscious roles. I understand them, I have deep compassion for them, and I'm committed to lending my Self energy to help them now. Together we can explore how to build the muscle of choice, how to make it an integral part of your daily life, and how, by choosing the simplicity of the check-in process, you'll offer the presence of Self to your Firefighter parts that work so hard trying to protect you from your exiled past. This is a practice that requires devotion, commitment, and a desire to feel free.

Cece Sykes says, "Healing is Self-led decisions over and over again."

The simplicity of this concept can be the key to grappling with addiction. Small steps toward long-term transformation are far more possible than overnight success, and they offer a comforting approach to the journey of recovery. In my early days of sobriety, I had a friend named Joel who imparted this wisdom to me. He had 10 years of sobriety, a beautiful apartment, considerable success, and awesome friends; his life was great. Curious about his path to this point, I asked for his guidance. His response was simple: "Lots of little right actions." I took his words to heart and dedicated myself to this philosophy, committing to small, consistent steps to support my recovery journey. Today, 19 years later (at the time of writing), I remain clean and sober. It's a testament to the power of consistently embracing those little right actions, which, over time, can bring about radical change.

Let's take a first small action now and safely check in with a Firefighter. As always, if you experience any hesitation or observe another Manager emerging, please prioritize the well-being of your internal parts and revisit this at a time that feels more emotionally stable.

This check-in is *not* designed to deeply explore your Firefighters but rather to guide you toward a Self-led perception of them. Simply choosing to see the Firefighter as part of you, rather than as you, can offer great relief.

Start with a choice. **Choose to check in** with a Firefighter part with the aim of seeing it through the lens of Self and recognizing its true intentions. The beauty of taking this step, especially when dealing with a Firefighter, is that by recognizing it as a part, you create an opportunity for a relationship instead of assigning blame. Seeing your Firefighter as a part is a profound act of Self-compassion in its own right.

Become **curious**. Once you've focused your attention inward toward the Firefighter, gently offer a series of questions. These questions are designed to create a sense of respect and openness toward the part.

Begin by taking note of where you feel the Firefighter's presence in your body. Offer it some breath, and allow it to express itself.

Then ask the part:

- How are you trying to help me?
- How long have you tried to help in this way?
- When you try to stop, what happens?
- What are you afraid would happen if you stopped protecting in this way?

These questions are designed to open your heart to witnessing the Firefighter's positive intentions, allowing more Self energy to come through. Offering your Firefighter this gentle inquiry gives it a newfound respect and compassionate connection rather than shame and blame.

Compassionately connect by placing your hand on your heart and offer this statement to the part:

I recognize how hard you're trying to protect me. I'm not here to manage or control you, I just want to connect.

Now check for C qualities of Self. Notice if you have an experience of any C qualities of Self. If you feel called, write with the part, allowing it to respond by writing whatever comes forward. Pick up a notebook and journal your response.

CHOICE RATHER THAN FORCE

In my own addiction recovery, I've found that the more I proactively connect to the Firefighter parts, the more compassion becomes natural. I've committed to creating relationships rather than control. When I aim to establish a relationship, I strip away the shame/blame cycle and open up to a whole new pattern—a pattern that has the power to heal. When we repeat new behavior and establish new habitual patterns, we have the power to change the neural pathways in our brain. I've personally found that when new patterns come through choice rather than force, they are much more likely to stick and have an innate power to change my beliefs. Choosing to check in with a Firefighter in this way creates a new Self-directed pattern. Each subtle shift toward a Self-compassionate perspective on a Firefighter offers it a chance to become free from shame and truly be seen. No amount of shame or blame will help a Firefighter get out of its extreme role. It's a relational connection that provides a real chance for long-lasting healing.

The more access we have to Self, the more we know where to turn for help. Self becomes an internal sponsor, always available to listen, learn, and hold space for the Firefighter no matter how extreme it may become. One compassionate connection at a time creates lasting change inside.

Nineteen years into my journey of sobriety, it's evident how Self has been a constant presence. The gentle whisper of Self played a pivotal role in guiding me on a path toward recovery. The ever-present Self energy and my willingness are what have kept me sober one day at a time.

CHAPTER 10

SELF-FORGIVENESS

Early in my career, I immersed myself in the spiritual perspectives of forgiveness. This is because forgiveness has the ability to catalyze miraculous shifts in our lives. It liberates us, allowing us to dwell in the present moment, released from the burdens of past shame and the fears of the future. This state of freedom is where our true shift occurs—we reclaim our innocence, our light, and our inner harmony. This is the true meaning of Self-forgiveness.

Forgiveness isn't an action we take, it's an experience we have. An experience that is available to all of us when we open our hearts to Self to help us heal and set free our Protector parts. "How can I possibly forgive myself?" is a phrase I've heard countless times over the years. My response is clear—all that's required is your willingness to forgive. The slightest willingness opens the door for the possibility of forgiveness to set in.

When we remain driven by our Protectors, we're stuck in the past. We repeat the same roles, activating feelings of shame that make us blame ourselves for falling back into old habits. Have you ever found yourself in full-blown Self-attack, blaming and shaming yourself for your actions?

Maybe you wake up hungover and can't remember what you did the night before. You find yourself filled with the shame that you fell back into the alcohol addiction cycle. The shame and blame become so extreme that the only way to feel better is to pick up again to numb out the other Protectors. This shame cycle keeps us stuck in the loop of our Protectors, which blocks the opportunity to experience forgiveness. But the willingness to forgive offers our parts the chance to choose again—to choose to check in. The desire to forgive your Protector parts is all that's required to begin the journey.

I embarked on the journey of self-forgiveness early in my sobriety, guided by the Self energy of my sponsor, who always extended forgiveness to me. It didn't matter what I needed to share with her; she consistently responded with forgiveness. Whether I'd done something truly shameful, acted poorly in a relationship, or encountered challenges with my recovery—her unwavering response was "You can forgive yourself." At that time I may not have known how to forgive myself, but her words alone were sufficient for forgiveness to pierce through the shame. Her Self energy and dedication to forgiveness provided the support I needed to release myself from the guilt and shame cycle.

SELF-FORGIVENESS IS A SPIRITUAL EXPERIENCE

Over time my sponsor's ability to see my addictive parts through the lens of forgiveness rubbed off on me. I embraced the relief of what it was like to let my part off the hook and give her space to be held in love. When I began applying the check-in process with my addict part, I started to experience spontaneous moments of Self-forgiveness. One time in a meditation I saw her standing before me; she was crying and desperate. I felt my heart open as intuitive words came through me: "I forgive you, Gabby." This spontaneous surge of Self-compassion and connection flooded my entire body. Relief came over my addict part's face, her forehead softened, and she took a deep breath. Feeling connected to Self, she was able to be released from the shame of the past and set free. This powerful vision allowed me to see all the shameful things I'd done and the burdens I'd carried in a whole new light—through a new lens of compassion. In this spontaneous moment of Self-acceptance, I could see the addict part with love and respect the role she'd played in my life. I felt the part soften inside me as Self energy guided forgiveness to set in.

While a spontaneous spiritual awakening of Self-forgiveness may feel far from reach, trust that throughout this book you have been taking radical steps toward it. Each time you've checked in with your parts, you've strengthened the bridge to Self. As you continue to do so, your Self-connection grows, and so does your awareness of the motivation behind your Protectors. In time it becomes easier to recognize that parts possess only positive intentions—to protect us in some capacity. While you may not fully accept your parts right away, note the moments when you recognize their positive intentions. Developing this perspective on your parts will help you begin to establish a compassionate relationship with them, allowing for greater possibilities of Self-forgiveness. Again, you don't have to force forgiveness between the part and Self—it has the power to happen spontaneously. (It may surprise you to learn that this is measurable: it's been shown that when people are led through IFS-inspired self-forgiveness meditations, they report an increased capacity to forgive—not only themselves, but others.[1])

A sign that Self-forgiveness has set in is when you no longer feel ashamed of your Protector. You may have compassion for the part or see it more clearly through the understanding of its intentions. You may feel more connected inside and open to creative ways of changing patterns. The C qualities of Self arise naturally, and as they develop, Self-forgiveness can come through.

NEW AND VALUABLE ROLES

Self-forgiveness offers parts the chance to take on new and valuable roles in our inner and outer world. The 25-year-old part of me, the cocaine addict, is an important part of who I am today—I hold her with deep reverence. Damn, she worked hard. Through the lens of Self-forgiveness, I can see how hard she worked to keep me safe, and for that, I love her, have compassion for her, and am grateful for her. I can see clearly that while she caused a lot of suffering, she played a significant role in my life. Looking back at her past extreme behaviors, I now view her through the lens of compassion, understanding that she had only positive intentions to shield me from an exiled part I was not ready to face.

As I write this book, she has been sober for 19 years. She's no longer burdened by her extreme addiction and can now direct her energy as a force for good. She thrives on being clear and in control and accomplishing a lot. Her productivity surpasses most people's—she can achieve in a day what takes others far longer. She's a super producer! She possesses an extraordinary ability to energize and inspire a room filled with thousands of people. Her high vibration is infectious. Now that she feels safe and trusts Self, she can use her passionate energized qualities as a source of good in the world.

This is the essence of Self-forgiveness: instead of shaming away your parts, you acknowledge and value their roles, guiding them to harness their strengths for positive purposes.

FORGIVING A PART HAS A DOMINO EFFECT

We have many parts of us living at odds inside our internal family system. Parts are at odds and interconnected at the same time; therefore, when one part is triggered, others become activated. The same is true for a part that becomes connected to Self—if one part experiences Self-forgiveness, other Protector parts can borrow the benefits of that connection. Self begets more Self.

I witnessed this ripple effect in my own inner world. As I became more and more comfortable forgiving my drug addict part, Self-compassion toward other lingering addictive parts set in. For instance, whenever I'd become controlling or obsessive at work (another Protector), I'd notice a shameful part trying to take over. This part would attempt to shame me for acting out or getting flooded in front of my employees. With my newfound Self-forgiveness muscle, I was able to naturally initiate the check-in process with a willingness to forgive. As more Self energy flowed through me, I could sense an openhearted feeling emerging organically. This heightened awareness enabled the process of Self-forgiveness for every part within me. I softened toward all parts, expressing respect and gratitude for the significant roles they've played in my life. Forgiving one part set off a ripple effect.

FORGIVENESS IS BESTOWED UPON US

My husband, Zach, edits all of my books. This collaboration is a gift for both of us. I get a great edit and he gets the opportunity to test-drive my newest ideas for living a more fulfilling life. For years I'd talked to him about IFS, offering suggestions, wanting to help him connect inward. I was always met with the same resistance: "I'm happy it's working for you, it's just not for me." But now something shifted, and throughout the process of editing this book, I noticed Zach became more and more curious about his parts. He'd ask me questions or mention casually that he tried checking in with a part. Then one afternoon when I was away on work, I received a call from Zach. "My back is really bothering me. Do you think we can check in with it?" I did my best not to scream YESSSS through the phone—I was so excited to share this process with him.

We dedicated 30 minutes to checking in with Zach's back pain as various other Protectors surfaced. A particular Protector got his attention: self-judgment. As he extended curiosity toward the judgmental part, he discovered it had been a constant presence in his life. As I witnessed this clarity spark within him, I harnessed my Self energy and asked, "How do you feel now?"

After a moment of silence, he responded, "I feel relieved—I can let myself off the hook."

He went on, "I'm recognizing for the first time that this judgment isn't a thing that I need to carry around. It's suppressing a deep-rooted feeling from my childhood that I should address."

I inhaled deeply, allowing the wisdom of Self to flow through my words. "Exactly, my love. Your awareness is the key—it opens your heart to this part, inviting Self to help."

Zach's courage to check in and become aware of who was inside was enough for him to open his heart and let Self help. The words "I feel relieved—I can let myself off the hook" were a spontaneous healing moment for Zach because for the first time he was able to forgive a part that had been running his life for so many years. He could separate the part from himself and recognize its value in keeping him safe. In doing so, he could un-blend from the part, allowing relief to set in. His back pain could subside and the calm presence of Self could offer spontaneous Self-forgiveness. This was a miracle, and a pinnacle turning point in Zach's life.

This miracle of Self-forgiveness is available to you too. You don't have to force it or figure anything out. By following the check-in process outlined in this chapter, you'll send a message to your parts that Self-forgiveness is possible. The promise of this practice is increased Self-awareness and an easier access to a sense of inner safety and genuine healing. When a part is acknowledged for its hard work, it can release the burden of shame and instead respect its role in the internal system. When the underlying motivation behind the Protector is brought to the forefront, the part no longer needs to do what it was doing.

Forgiving parts is ultimately an intuitive inner experience that spontaneously occurs. Through the check-in process, I will guide you now to open your heart to the spiritual experience of forgiving a part. When we shift our perception of our parts, we receive miraculous relief and a whole new perception of ourselves. Please consider that Self-forgiveness may feel far from reach at this time. It's highly possible that your parts may even still be resisting the idea that Self is inside. Don't focus on the outcome of the exercise; rather, trust that opening your consciousness to the possibility of Self-forgiveness is enough to set the wheels in motion.

Forgiveness doesn't happen overnight—it's a natural connection that can be nurtured over time. Remember, parts have deeply ingrained trauma, resistance, fear, shame, and lack of trust in Self. The idea of forgiving a part (especially an extreme Firefighter) can bring up fear and anxiety for some individuals. This may be due to the vulnerability and openness required to connect with these parts. Some parts may be overwhelmed by feelings of shame or guilt for falling back into or staying stuck in extreme or unconscious behavior. When parts are stuck in extreme and protective roles, it's hard to see their true intentions—which are to protect you. Keep this in mind as you follow the steps in this chapter. There are likely parts of you that will stand in the way of Self-forgiveness, unwilling to let you off the hook. Do your best to be the witness of whatever comes up and remain patient in the process. Keep in mind that even contemplating the idea of forgiving an overly extreme part will be triggering. Therefore, once again, I do not recommend you apply this practice to Exiles or Firefighters. Choose to work with a part that feels less extreme in your life.

YOU CAN CHOOSE FORGIVENESS OVER FEAR

Take a moment now to turn your attention inward and tap into a Protector part that's been around for a while. Once you have a sense of connection to that part, ask, "Am I willing to forgive this part?" Notice the response. Maybe you hear a resounding "Hell no!" or maybe you notice a sensation of openness. Follow your own inner guidance and determine if you feel ready to check in. As always, if it feels too soon or too overwhelming, just read the practice without following the steps. To listen to the guided audio of this practice, go to DearGabby.com/SelfHelpResources.

If you notice even the slightest willingness to forgive a part, take a moment now to **choose to check in**. Remember, all you need is the willingness to forgive to set the spiritual process in motion. Connect inside, offering up the willingness to forgive to any part that is present inside you now. Focus on a part that needs your attention, and when you're ready, take the next step of curiosity.

Open your heart to the part by offering **curiosity**. Ask the part the following questions:

- How old are you? Do you have a gender? Are there any thoughts, feelings, or sensations you want me to be aware of?
- What is your role in my internal system?
- Are you trying to protect me?
- How long have you had this role?
- Do you like this role?
- If you were no longer in this role, what else might you be doing?
- How does it feel to think about that?
- Do you feel a strong emotion, or tension, or pain? Do you feel numb?
- Is there anything else you want me to know?

Then place both your hands on your heart and focus your attention on the feelings and sensations inside, offering a safe space for the part to be witnessed with love.

Next, **compassionately connect** to the part by **exploring the part's positive intentions**. Take a moment now to consider the part's positive intentions and devotion to you.

Open your heart to a deeper understanding of its role and function in your internal system.

- Take a moment to reflect on how hard the Protector has been working to shield you from your Exiles.
- Acknowledge its positive intentions—it's been trying to protect or serve you in some way, even if its actions haven't always been helpful.
- Notice if you feel any C qualities arise, and offer them up to the part by simply letting it know how you feel.
- Offer the part your presence. Just sit with the feelings inside and any thoughts or emotions that come forward. Give it space.

WRITE A LETTER TO THE PART

Take this practice a step further by opening your journal to write to the part. Before you begin, connect to the Self energy that is available to you. Feel into the feelings of Self and allow that energy to guide this writing exercise. Open your heart more and write a letter to the part, allowing the supportive and compassionate energy of Self to take the lead. As you write, reflect on how hard the part has worked to keep you safe and how scared it must be. Open up your conscious awareness of Self as you write freely, focusing energy toward the important role the part has played in your life. Let Self lead the way.

When you feel complete, gently place your hand on your heart once again and take a moment to read over what came through. Focus your attention now toward any C qualities of Self that are present in the writing, in your body, or in your mind. Then check in again.

- How do you feel toward the part now?
- Does the part notice that Self is there? Does it feel Self energy?
- Does the part trust Self at this moment?
- Do you feel a stronger Self-to-part connection?

Take a moment to document how you feel, or simply sit with the feeling and allow it to permeate your being.

If you weren't able to feel a connection to Self during this exercise, trust that your curiosity and willingness to practice the exercise were enough to let a molecule of Self come through. Practice patience and embrace the unfolding of this process—rather than forcing the part to connect to Self, allow the connection to naturally reveal itself. Self-connection creates the opportunity for forgiveness to set in, but this can take time. Therefore, bring your newfound willingness to forgive your parts into your dedicated check-in process. Let Self guide you through the steps provided. The secret to Self-forgiveness is to surrender and let Self reveal the shift.

THE PROMISE OF FORGIVENESS

I promise the more you commit to the daily habit of checking in with your parts, the easier it will be to experience Self-forgiveness. Your willingness to forgive and check in will guide you toward a new way of living. You'll know a whole new level of trust inside—a trust that develops more over time. Each time you genuinely acknowledge, honor, and respect a part for its role, you offer it the opportunity to feel safe and respected—to be forgiven. This safe connection is all it needs to trust that it can be forgiven, settle, and ultimately take on a new valuable role inside. Keep this connection going by staying open and willing to forgive your parts each time you let Self in. Remind your part that you're not there to change it but to help it. Then when you naturally forgive one part, it will become easier to relate to your other parts in the same way.

SELF-FORGIVENESS IN ACTION

My ability to forgive my parts has offered me clarity and understanding toward them. As I un-blend from parts and create a stronger Self-connection, I have a greater awareness of how their behavior affects others. I witnessed this recently when attending a mastermind—a professional mentoring group—with fellow authors. In group settings, I often have a "bossy" part that shows up wanting to grab the microphone and start leading the session. From the moment I walked through the door of this mastermind, this bossy part was in high gear, interrupting the speakers with questions, offering unsolicited advice, and totally monopolizing the conversation.

As the day came to an end, I noticed shame brewing inside. Attempting to deflect this discomfort, I made lighthearted remarks to my fellow attendees, such as "You know me, I can get super aggressive" or jesting, "I feel like I've been yelling at everyone for an hour!" These jokes served as a protective mechanism, a way to silence the relentless inner critic that was spiraling into shame.

I left the event early in an effort to avoid any further awkward or embarrassing moments. Arriving home, I was plagued by a sense of lingering shame—like a hangover from the day's events, as if I had regressed into old habits that no longer served me. Rather than succumbing to the burden of shame, I consciously connected with the "fixer" part that had been so controlling early in the day. I spent time checking in with the part, connecting through curiosity.

As I delved deeper, I opened my heart to feelings of compassion, asking the part, "What do you need?" In response it whispered, "I need forgiveness." I took a moment to inhale deeply, placing my hand over my heart, and exhaled, feeling a profound sense of relief wash over me. In that very instant, I remembered that I possessed the capacity to extend forgiveness instead of judgment. I could *choose* to let her off the hook by viewing her through a compassionate lens. I realized that, although it may exhibit moments of assertiveness (and possibly piss people off), it ultimately carries positive intentions and a loving heart. I could see that while this part can be intense, it's also the part of me that is able to command a stage, fearlessly offer advice to audiences, and teach with authority. I was able to see the part with compassion for her need to be seen and simultaneously extend her gratitude for her supportive role. The shame melted as a new perspective set in and Self-forgiveness naturally unfolded.

This story exemplifies that forgiveness is a bestowed gift that becomes available to us when we are willing to receive it. So the next time you find yourself judging or criticizing a part, start the check-in process with the affirmation "I'm willing to forgive this part and see it through the lens of love." Self-forgiveness allows your parts to be witnessed through compassion rather than judgment. The expectation isn't that you'll never fall back into old patterns but that you'll feel empowered to forgive the part and choose again. Forgiveness offers parts clarity and compassion, allowing them to become less extreme and to use their gifts for good. It's not that I want to get rid of my "bossy"; I just want to let Self help her show up in calm and valuable ways.

PARTS CAN BE PRESENT ALONGSIDE SELF

Earlier in this book, I introduced a Protector that I call "knives out." This part would become defensive at any perceived character assault. As I've become more connected to Self, the part has significantly mellowed. Yet just an hour before writing this passage, my "knives out" part was dramatically reactivated.

I had some issues with the front desk at my doctor's office. This was especially frustrating because I felt so dependent on my doctor. A misunderstanding about billing led to an urgent and aggressive phone call from them demanding immediate payment. This accusatory approach, lacking any sensitivity, hit a nerve related to my past—a child part that grew up with financial insecurity.

In my adult life I've compensated for this by always making it a point to pay on time. So when the doctor's office called, it triggered a defensive reaction in me. Rage and tears came through the phone as I defended my actions and pointed out that their processes needed serious improvement.

After I hung up the phone, I felt a sense of calm. I wasn't embarrassed by my reaction. In fact, I felt somewhat proud for standing up for myself, which is something I wouldn't have been able to do before.

As the Universe would have it, the moment I hung up the phone, Dick Schwartz called me to say hello. I answered the phone with "Good timing, my friend!" Then I immediately launched in with a question to Dick that I had been mulling over. "If a Protector part shows up when you're genuinely trying to look after yourself, is that necessarily a bad thing? Does it mean the Self isn't present?" He laughed and replied, "The part is there with Self. You might not be so blended with that part that it completely overwhelms you; there might still be a connection to the Self shining through."

His answer made me realize the value of the time I'd spent getting to know "knives out." On the phone, rather than becoming entirely fused with her, I allowed her to look after me while still feeling the presence of my Self energy. I was somewhat intertwined with the part, but not entirely consumed by it. "Knives out" didn't dominate the scene; rather, she stepped in to protect me in the best way she knew how at that moment, with Self energy simultaneously present.

An hour later, I checked in with "knives out" and asked her what she needed. Her response was clear: "I need to make amends to the lady at the front desk." It wasn't coming from a place of shame or regret, but from a desire for mutual respect. I could see that the part knew it was right to stand up, offer candid feedback, and look after me. She recognized the importance of her protective role, yet she was also aware of the less than tactful way she had delivered the message. She invited Self in to help her make amends—and that's precisely what she did.

Through my devotion to Self-forgiveness, "knives out" plays an important part in my life today. This once-extreme part—now connected to Self—has the ability to confidently speak her truth and courageously hold strong boundaries. This shift is so profound that I've even renamed the part. Today, I refer to her as a boundary part that takes care of my needs.

FORGIVING OTHER PEOPLE'S PARTS

Something super cool happens when you get into the swing of forgiving your own parts; it becomes easier to forgive the parts in others. Recently I've noticed that certain things my husband does that once triggered me now activate curiosity and compassion. Instead of saying, "What's wrong?" in an accusatory tone, I'll ask, "Do you need some help?" This genuine inquiry and adjustment in my energy offers his activated parts respect, compassion, and the ability to speak up. Even if he's deeply blended with a part and can't connect in that moment, I can stay in Self and hold space for his experience. And he can do the same for me, allowing for a more naturally Self-led relationship.

Seeing people as a multitude of parts offers you the ability to create deep and meaningful connections. I cannot count the number of times in my life when I've been hit with negative energy by a stranger (someone on the street, a cashier at the store, a person on a Zoom call) and instead of meeting their resistance, I respond with love. My choice to extend Self energy to others has allowed their parts to soften right before my eyes. I once heard my late friend and mentor Dr. Wayne Dyer say in a lecture, "See the light in others, and treat them as if that is all you see." Choosing to see the light in yourself expands your capacity to see the light in others. By connecting to your parts and compassionately understanding your own suffering, you can more easily recognize the suffering of others. Instead of shaming them, you can naturally choose to see them through the lens of Self—through the lens of light.

Here's a recent example to illustrate the point. During a workshop that I conducted the venue's event planner walked around with "resting bitch face" and could barely look me in the eye. At first my parts were kicked up by her overall vibe, but instead of letting her vibe get me down, I chose to check in. Engaging in the check-in process, I connected to the activated part within me. As I finished the process, I heard an inner intuitive voice come forth: "See her as a spiritual assignment—see her with love." With Self's guidance, this single check-in completely transformed my day. Once I knew I was truly connected to Self energy, I made a commitment to genuinely radiate it toward her throughout the day. During the lunch break, I approached the event planner with questions about her life, infused with a sincere curiosity. Later on when I saw her revert back to low-vibe mode, I silently sent her a prayer.

As the day went on, her energy seemed to lighten, and she even cracked a joke. After the workshop concluded, she approached me in the greenroom. "Gabby, I struggle with serious social anxiety, and sometimes it's challenging for me to perform my job. But today, for some reason, I felt so connected to you, and that really put me at ease. Thank you." Wow, what a miracle. My Self energy facilitated her access to her own sense of calm—her own authentic Self.

I am fortunate to have the opportunity to engage in these kinds of experiences daily, all because I've made it a habit to check in with my parts and realign with Self. By recognizing the light within my own parts, I can embrace Wayne's wisdom. I see the light in others and treat them as if that is all I see.

Never underestimate the challenges someone might be confronting. Each person carries a collection of parts that remain vigilant and on high alert, ready to protect them when they're triggered. Viewing the human condition through this lens helps shine light on the source of their suffering. When we as individuals cultivate a trusting connection between our parts and Self—forgiving our parts—we cultivate empathy and compassion toward others. Establishing a collective energy of Self, we shift the energy throughout the world. Never underestimate the power of your individual connection to Self.

A NOTE FOR EMPATHS

I want to shine a light for empaths who are reading this. You might catch yourself thinking about the parts in others you'd wish to befriend. Take a moment to notice that longing, and turn your attention toward the part of you that puts serving others over serving yourself. The only way to truly be an expression of Self energy for others is to embody it from within. If you're looking to make a positive impact on the world, the first step is to realign with your genuine Self. Remember, this book is called *Self Help,* not *How to Help Everyone Else.* Pay attention to the parts within that want to override your own healing journey in an effort to try to heal someone else.

SHARING HARD TRUTHS FROM SELF

When we experience the power of witnessing our Protectors, we can more easily see them in others. At our core we all want the same thing: authentic love and connection. To love and be loved—that's it. Loving every part of who you are allows you to soften toward the parts in others. I know this might sound like a quote on a tapestry at a yoga studio, but today I can say with all my heart that these words are true: to truly be loved comes when we learn to love every part inside. This is the true meaning of self-love.

Forgiving a part is the greatest act of self-love and allows for a deep sense of safety and peace to set in. When we let our parts off the hook and compassionately connect inward, we send a message to all of our parts inside that they are loved. **The true antidote to our internal suffering comes when we love and accept all our parts.** To be loved is to love every part of who you are.

Forgiving our parts enables us to perceive both ourselves and others with understanding. The profound experience of Self-forgiveness will not only open your heart but also grant you a life enriched with greater meaning and serenity. I'd like to conclude this chapter by sharing a quote from Dick Schwartz that beautifully encapsulates this sentiment: "As we embrace and love all aspects of ourselves, we can extend that love to all of humanity, and in doing so, play a part in healing the world."

CHAPTER 11

SELF-TRUST

Recently I skipped an entire month of therapy due to my travel schedule. When the sessions resumed, I said to my therapist, "Ya know, no offense but I feel really great even without our sessions."

"That's because you're practicing 'Self' help," she replied.

She was right! With more trust in Self, I could turn inward for support. Self could be the internal leader I could rely on. This didn't take away the value of my therapy, it just enhanced it. I could tend to my parts anywhere and anytime while feeling guided and supported. I was never alone in my suffering.

I wasn't aware of it at the time, but I instinctively began tapping into Self throughout the day. Sometimes only for fleeting moments—but that didn't matter. What counted was that these repeated connections were fostering a feeling of inner safety.

When I felt triggered, I'd instinctively step aside and check in, exploring the part and its underlying thoughts and emotions. I'd get curious, flushing out more of these feelings. Then I'd lean on compassionate connection, inquiring what it needed. Once I noticed C qualities of Self inside, I'd naturally witness the part soften and an inner sensation of safety and ease set in. This daily check-in became habitual and instinctual.

My commitment to and daily repetition of the check-in process helped me become less reactive and more present and compassionate toward every part of me. With consistent connection inward, I no longer had to speak *as* my parts but instead *for* my parts. Of course, there are times when I can feel flooded by a part, but Self is still with me. I can be in the part, allowing it space to act out, scream, or speak out, all the while knowing that Self is present with the part, holding space for it to be seen and heard. The goal has never been to avoid freaking out or having extreme emotions, but to allow my parts to freely express their needs. Constant contact with parts allows them to feel free inside to get the help they need.

INTEGRATION

This conversation with my therapist helped me see how integrated my internal family system had become. All my parts were working together in harmony, allowing space for Self to come forward and support the activated feelings. I could see that through my connection to Self, my Protectors didn't have to take over. The controller part could show up at work and Self would be there to help. The fearful part could express its needs and Self would be present to hear them. When I felt defensive, the boundary part I used to call "knives out" would arise and I'd naturally breathe into the feelings, clearing space to check in. Above all, I could observe all these parts with connection, trusting that Self was caring for all my parts. With this trust in Self, all my parts could peacefully coexist without overpowering one another. When my internal family of Protector parts gained trust in Self, they no longer tried to take over—instead they trusted that Self was always there to help. No part got in the way of this connection, and everyone was on board to let Self help.

IFS calls this experience *integration*. It happens by fostering a sense of cooperation, understanding, and collaboration among the parts in the internal family system. Instead of parts being in conflict with one another, they can be more balanced and harmonious, establishing a healthy relationship among them.

Experiencing this integration allowed me to feel firsthand what it was like to have all parts trust in Self. While parts could still get activated, none of them took over. Instead they could freely feel their feelings and express their needs while allowing Self to help. They trusted that Self could care for them. I experienced the miracle of IFS: inner balance and harmony. When parts are in harmony and inner conflict is resolved, we can calmly navigate life (and its challenges). When parts work together with Self as the leader, anything is possible.

SELF-TRUST LEADS TO BALANCE AND HARMONY

Each moment of connection to Self helps you establish more Self-trust. Like any relationship, Self-trust takes time and repetition of behavior. The more you check in, the more you build trust. I imagine you've experienced moments of trusting Self along the way. Maybe you felt an inner sense of calm that helped you make an important decision. Or maybe you sensed the presence of compassion for a part, allowing you to let the part off the hook. Each encounter with Self sends a message to your brain that you are safe, there's help inside, and you're not alone. These subtle moments add up, and in time Self-trust and connection are realized and inner balance sets in. Your parts are in harmony with Self.

We're all looking for balance and harmony in our life. And we try to get there with the gym or yoga, meditation, or me-time. What I've grown to know is that these one-off events may offer a temporary relief to an otherwise stressful life, but they are *not* the path to balance. Balance comes when our inner world is in harmony. Self-trust allows you to feel faithful and directed by a calm, connected presence inside. Even in the face of challenging life events or setbacks, you always know there's safety inside. The secret to living with balance is to trust in Self.

I've also witnessed this balance with a friend. Her inner balance grew as she practiced the check-in process, making it easier to connect to Self energy. For years she struggled with an "overachiever part" that showed up in every area of her life—parenting, work, romance, and even her exercise routine. In time, with her devotion to the check-in process, she was able to reconnect with Self, which allowed her to finally release her dependence on external validation for safety. She noticed that her "overachiever part" no longer sought others' approval to feel worthy, which calmed her controlling tendencies. Without the pressure to achieve in order to feel safe, her "people-pleaser part" eased up. Each Self-connection provided her parts with the trust needed to relax. With Self energy present, her parts could calm, giving her a sense of balance that reshaped her attitude, energy, and life.

True balance emerges from inner harmony and security, not from external changes. When you feel safe inside and trust in Self, you can move through life with more ease. Your inner safety offers you the courage to take risks, the clarity to create change, and the calmness to find a way through every block. When you trust in Self, you live a guided life.

ADDRESS ANY RESISTANCE TO TRUSTING SELF

Trusting in Self is often hard at first. Protectors don't believe they're safe to trust in anyone, let alone an invisible inner presence. But the existence of hope is enough to cut through the barrier of protection. My stories, the words in this book, and the fact that Self qualities are proven to improve people's lives in tangible ways—from better sleep to better relationships to a stronger sense of worth[1]—all offer your pragmatic Protectors not only hope but proof that Self-help works. Let's take a moment to suspend any limiting beliefs that hold you back from trusting in Self.

This check-in process is designed to help you get to know any parts that are resisting Self. This is an opportunity to offer these resistant parts a chance to express any concerns they may have about trusting Self. Throughout the book you've gained greater and greater awareness of your Protectors, which inherently means that you've established a sense of separation from them. For instance, when my husband was able to reach out and check in with his back pain, rather than become overtaken by the pain, he could see his back as a Protector. Like Zach, I expect that you too have had moments of witnessing your parts as separate from you—as Protectors. Each time you've chosen to check in, it has initiated Self energy in the form of curiosity or openness toward these parts. Therefore, I can say with certainty that you have indeed experienced glimmers of Self.

Do your parts wholeheartedly trust Self? In my experience, building trust in Self comes when we add up one small connection at a time. One check-in, one prayer to ask Self for help, one journaling exercise, one meditation. One moment of witnessing a part each day builds up a new muscle inside, deepening more and more faith in Self.

Our final check-in together is designed to honor any parts that may still resist Self. A powerful way to build trust is by telling the truth. In this check-in process, I'll guide your parts to experience their resistance to Self, notice it, honor it, and give voice to it. This truth is valuable information and important to any relationship. Establishing a trusting Self-to-part relationship—a relationship that will support you forever—requires clarity. Right here, right now, we can let your parts voice any fears and concerns about letting Self help.

CHECK IN

If you feel called to practice at this time, **choose to check in** with any part that does not yet trust Self. (Keep in mind that it's possible that none of your parts trust Self yet.)

Next, become **curious** about this part. Take a moment to notice where it lives in your body.

Is there a feeling, emotion, or thought attached to it?

Focusing your attention toward that part, offer it some curiosity questions:

- Are you aware the Self is here?
- If so, how do you feel toward Self?
- Do you have hope that Self can help?
- Or do you resist trusting that Self-connection is even possible?

- Have you ever sensed a glimmer of Self in a moment of flow or throughout the journey of this book?

Take your time to become even more curious by asking any additional questions that come through naturally.

Once you're able to witness the part as an observer, you'll know you're ready to extend **compassionate connection**. Take out a pen and journal and freely allow the part to respond to the following questions:

- Are you aware that Self is here?

Take a moment to listen and respond.

- Can you sense into any resistance to letting Self in?
- Describe any feelings, thoughts, or sensations of resistance.
- What do you need to trust more in Self?

Listen and respond.

- If you could trust in Self to take care of you, how might you feel?
- Allow the responses to come through.
- What burdened beliefs, feelings, energies, or emotions would you like to offer up to Self?

Respond naturally.

Check for any C qualities of Self. Following the final question, notice if any qualities of Self came through in response to the question: *How does Self feel toward you?*

Did you notice any Cs: compassion, connection, curiosity, creativity, courage, calm, clarity, confidence? Upon reflection take a moment to notice if there's a deeper sense of Self inside.

If you feel even the slightest connection to Self, sense into what it feels like in your body.

- Do you feel more present?
- Are you breathing differently?
- Do you feel more clear?
- Do you feel an inner sense of wisdom, calmness, or compassion?
- Do you feel a sensation of trust?

Sit with these feelings for a moment, breathe into them, and give your parts a chance to feel Self energy. Sit and be still for as long as you like.

When you feel ready, you can reflect on the experience in your journal by documenting any glimmers of connection to Self that may have come through. Notice if your part feels ever so slightly less resistant to Self. Notice what you notice and document it now.

CONSCIOUS CONTACT WITH SELF

My hope is that this final check-in offers your parts space to allow even the slightest bit of resistance to melt away. Every glimmer of Self-connection counts. What's most important about building trust in Self is not how fast it happens but how simple you make it.

Check in for five minutes a day

Five minutes a day of checking in with a part allows the energy of Self to multiply inside your inner world. One check-in at a time opens your consciousness and your heart to receive Self-help and witness the shifts inside. One daily small turn inward has the power to develop an instinctual habit that *will* change your life.

Celebrate the Cs

Throughout the book I've shared many stories of how my faith in Self has healed my life. I am living proof that Self can help. While my stories can offer you hope, it's your own inner shifts that will build your trust in Self. Pay close attention to the glimmers of Self along the way and witness them adding up. I have a nightly practice of reflecting on my Self-connection from the day. I'll document moments of Self-led relief or experiences that used to be run by parts but are now more Self-led. I spend five minutes at night celebrating the Cs from the day. This practice has allowed me to pay close attention to my developing relationship to Self and the great shifts along the way. Each connection to Self is a miracle to be celebrated.

Consider keeping an evening journal to capture moments each day when you felt connected to Self. Reflect on a check-in process you used or a situation you navigated intuitively with ease. Dedicate time daily to acknowledge and celebrate these connections to Self.

Follow these two daily commitments and pay attention to the shifts that occur inside. Adding up the subtle shifts creates radical change. Keep it simple and consider practicing a five-minute check-in once a day. Your conscious contact with your parts allows more Self to be revealed.

SELF-LEADERSHIP

As I acquired a deepening of Self-connection and trust, the more my compassionate and wise parts evolved. As a result it became easier for me to bring that energy into my team leadership; even in my most triggering moments. At a team offsite, I taught my employees about IFS and introduced the check-in process with the intention of ultimately helping them speak *for* their parts. One particular employee really took to the exercise and was eager to learn more about the process.

Months later I was able to experience it using this process with her in real time. We got on a video call to discuss an issue we were having at work. Before we dove into the dialogue, I confidently and calmly said, "I have a super activated part that's up right now. This situation is really triggering." My employee smiled and thanked me for speaking up for the part. An instant energy of ease set the stage for the conversation. As we carried on, there were moments when the part became more triggered or sensitive. At one point I made a suggestion about how to handle the issue that unintentionally offended her. Noticing this, I spoke for it. "I'm so sorry if that offended you; that wasn't my intention." I could see a part in her was kicked up and she responded defensively to protect herself in the moment. After talking a bit more, we seemed to smooth it over and shortly afterward ended the call.

Five minutes later she sent me a Slack message, and the conversation went like this:

> Employee:♥ Thank you for acknowledging your parts today. It makes it easier for me to speak for mine. I realized I may have had a part that needed

to reaffirm my ability and then quickly realized that my part needed to chill a little.

Me: OMG how cool to speak for our parts! This is the magic of IFS Self-led leadership. It's so cool that you're willing to speak in parts!

Employee: How lucky we are! Look at the space you've created for us to feel comfortable to talk about those parts!

Me: Well mama I've got a lot of my own parts that are just learning how to settle:) I have to speak for them so I don't speak AS them:)

Employee: I love it! I really feel a connection to how you think and how your parts may show up and it's really allowing me to build things with you in mind and being able to communicate them back to you!

Me: This whole interaction is literally the best moment. It shows how seamless life can be if we speak for our parts. Issues and miscommunication can be resolved effortlessly.

This experience exemplifies Self in action. My ability to speak up and acknowledge my part at the top of the call allowed me to remain steady during the conversation. By witnessing my ability to speak for a part, my employee was able to do the same, resulting in this miraculous interaction. What might have previously resulted in silent resentment or an uncomfortable confrontation instead transformed into a bonding experience between two coworkers. We were able to see each other's parts with compassion, thereby establishing a deeper connection.

Imagine if your encounters with your coworkers could be like this. Think about how much time you would save! This goes for all your relationships. What if you could enter into any conflict and mindfully speak *for* your parts rather than *as* them? What if you had the ability to Self-soothe in the moment so that instead of flying off the handle, you were able to get your needs met? Think about it. Wouldn't it be nice to relate to others in this way? Well, my friend, this is what happens when you build trust in Self.

THE PROMISES OF TRUSTING SELF

The inner experience of trusting Self offers a multitude of promises. Self-compassion will come naturally, and you'll become the nonjudgmental witness of your parts and their needs. When parts become integrated with Self, you'll feel an open heart and curiosity about every part of who you are. When Self is in the lead, you'll naturally acknowledge and accept the part, recognizing its positive intentions, allowing space for the part to settle naturally.

Presence sets in

When you trust in Self, you become present and open to whatever parts arise. It becomes second nature to accept and honor the thoughts and emotions of your Protectors. You can witness your feelings and sensations and speak *for* them with ease.

Self manifests

One of the greatest benefits of Self-trust is that you strengthen your spiritual connection and faith in your intuition. In this peaceful and faithful state, you feel connected to a powerful force of energy within and around you. This force is magnetic and attracts its likeness. Your intuition expands, allowing you to feel as though you have an inner guidance system directing your life. Wild synchronicities begin to occur, and you feel as though your life becomes guided, directed, and purposeful.

Inner wisdom

Another promise of trusting Self is that you'll experience enhanced inner wisdom. You'll experience clarity about yourself, and you'll intuitively know how to make decisions and show up for life with ease. Consider this a strong intuition, an inner guidance, and a knowing. You'll learn to trust this inner wisdom and use it as a guide. This wisdom will come through in your meditation as an inspired thought or intuitive direction. You'll grow to rely on it as it becomes more and more natural to access.

Heightened sense of purpose

You'll feel a strong connection to your purpose. You'll release your parts' perception of you and instead become led by deeper meaning. With a greater sense of Self, you'll naturally want to serve and contribute to the greater whole. Seeing the world through the lens of Self lets love move through you naturally—this is your purpose.

Your outside world is reflected by your internal connection

With a greater trust in Self, situations that once caused a lot of drama in your life become easier to navigate. You naturally release dependency on addictive patterns and instead feel intuitively guided toward solutions. You can witness your feelings and sensations and speak *for* them with ease.

Inside you feel more safe, allowing for more external safety and connection in relationships.

You feel free

No longer blended with parts, you trust that there's always a way through every block by asking Self for help. You trust in your ability to support your parts by connecting inward for Self-led support. You're no longer the victim of your parts, you're the gentle witness allowing Self to help.

These promises are true. I've lived them and I can share them with confidence. With trust in Self, I can turn inward at any moment and surrender to the presence of inner wisdom that I've grown to rely on. I promise all this and more.

HOPE MERCHANT

At this moment I invite you to trust in my experience and lean on my faith. A spiritual transformation is within reach, a fundamental shift in your beliefs.

In IFS there is a term, *hope merchant*. The concept is that the IFS practitioner or therapist can be a purveyor of hope for the patient, offering them their own Self energy and genuine confidence that healing is possible and that inner harmony is available. I can be that for you—I can be your hope merchant. My genuine motivation behind why I continue to write books year after year is to offer you hope. I can't do the check-in process for you, and I'm not your therapist, but I can be your hope merchant. My intention is to help you borrow my faith in Self and trust that with your own commitment to the process, you *will* experience miraculous shifts.

I'm here to hold space for your transformation, and I'm proud of you for getting to this point. With every word of this book you read, you invite Self to emerge. Let my guidance and understanding of Self seep through these pages. Lean on my faith in the ever-present help from Self as you continue to navigate this journey.

THE UNBURDENING

As I find myself wrapping up the final edits of this book, I recognize this has been a challenging time for me with work pressure and numerous changes that are activating lots of Protector parts. Despite the difficulties, the experience has been remarkable because it has allowed me to witness firsthand the positive effects of my Self-help journey.

Even when navigating tough situations, I can now check in with my activated parts along the way. I no longer find myself blended with these parts; I remember that I have the choice to check in. Staying connected to Self, I feel safe inside even in the midst of outer turmoil. I experienced this profound transformation in real time this afternoon during a therapy session.

I decide to take my session over the phone while walking up the hill near my house. Over the course of the two-mile walk, I discuss a part of me that was triggered before our session. Together, my therapist and I engage in a check-in with that part.

I exclaim, "She's really pissed off and frustrated. There's an underlying sense of anxiety and a tinge of rage. Her throat is tight but she wants to scream. Why does she keep falling into the same pattern? She should have gotten over this by now."

Intrigued, my therapist says, "Tell me more about the anxiety."

I blurt out, "She's anxious because she's tired of this role. She doesn't want to handle everything or push so hard. She wants to be creative and flexible. She wants to ask for what she wants and walk away from the minutiae. She wants to be free."

"If she wasn't in this role of controlling, what else might she be doing?" asks my therapist.

"She'd be creating, writing, and channeling spirit live on a stage again. She'd be spiritually aligned and in the flow. That's all she wants now. She's done with the controlling role. It's over. She's ready to let it go!"

BOOM! There it is—my controlling part has finally surrendered. "It's over," I repeat.

This is a pinnacle turning point for me.

My therapist knows it too. She seizes the moment and said, "Wow, are you ready to release her? Check in with the controller. Are you ready to help her unburden from this role?"

"I'm so ready, yes, let's do it!" I reply.

"Great! Let's start by naming the burden and negative belief that you would like to let go."

"The burdened part I call the 'controller,' and she carries the belief that if I don't do it, no one will."

"How would you like to release this burden through a ceremonial process? Choose one of the natural elements as a symbol of letting go. This can be releasing to light, surrendering to water, burning in fire, burying in earth, blowing away with wind, or whatever feels right to the part," my therapist explains.

"Let's burn it!" I respond emphatically.

"Great. Close your eyes and imagine the burden leaving your body and being burned by the flames. Take your time to visualize it . . ." She pauses, then asks, "How does that feel?"

With a sigh of relief, I respond, "It feels free, and my heart is open."

"Beautiful. Now take a moment to focus on this new energy—the energy that is emerging within you. This energy was likely the original qualities of the part before it became burdened. Experience it now. How does it feel?"

"It feels joyful and free. I feel free."

At that moment, I release the controller part of me that has been present for nearly 40 years. I set her free from the burdens she's carried for so long.

Reaching the hilltop as our session ends, I find a bench under a tree with a view of a pond. I sit there, allowing myself the space to absorb and integrate the experience.

I check in. Noticing the buzzing energy within, my vision sharpens, and a tranquil sense of safety envelops me. The cycle of controlling thoughts breaks, leaving my mind at ease.

I sit with the part in stillness—she's calm now. Together we overlook the pond, nowhere to go and nothing to do. We rest.

ENDNOTES

Chapter 1

1. Richard C. Schwartz and Martha Sweezy, *Internal Family Systems Therapy*, 2nd ed. (New York: The Guilford Press, 2002).
2. Richard C. Schwartz, *No Bad Parts: How the Internal Family Systems Model Changes Everything* (Boulder, CO: Sounds True, 2021).

Chapter 3

1. Hilary B. Hodgdon et al., "Internal Family Systems (IFS) Therapy for Posttraumatic Stress Disorder (PTSD) among Survivors of Multiple Childhood Trauma: A Pilot Effectiveness Study," *Journal of Aggression, Maltreatment & Trauma* 31, no. 1 (December 27, 2021): 22–43, https://doi.org/10.1080/10926771.2021.2013375.
2. Mary A. Steinhardt et al., "The Development and Validation of a Scale for Measuring Self-Leadership," *Journal of Self Leadership* 1 (2003): 20–31, https://foundationifs.org/images/banners/pdf/Journal_for_Self_Leadership_Steinhardt.pdf.
3. Shelley A. Haddock et al., "The Efficacy of Internal Family Systems Therapy in the Treatment of Depression among Female College Students: A Pilot Study," *Journal of Marital and Family Therapy* 43, no. 1 (August 8, 2016): 131–44, https://doi.org/10.1111/jmft.12184.
4. Hodgdon et al., "Internal Family Systems Therapy."
5. Anne Böckler et al., "Know Thy Selves: Learning to Understand Oneself Increases the Ability to Understand Others," *Journal of Cognitive Enhancement* 1, no. 2 (May 16, 2017): 197–209, https://doi.org/10.1007/s41465-017-0023-6.
6. Nancy A. Shadick et al., "A Randomized Controlled Trial of an Internal Family Systems-Based Psychotherapeutic Intervention on Outcomes in Rheumatoid Arthritis: A Proof-of-Concept Study,"

The Journal of Rheumatology 40, no. 11 (August 15, 2013): 1831–41, https://doi.org/10.3899/jrheum.121465.

7. François Le Doze, "IFS Applied to Migraine Management: Two Case Reports," *Journal of Self Leadership* 2 (2006): 37–43.

Chapter 6

1. Richard Schwartz, "The Larger Self," IFS Institute, https://ifs-institute.com/resources/articles/larger-self.

Chapter 8

1. Veronika Engert et al., "Specific Reduction in Cortisol Stress Reactivity after Social but Not Attention-Based Mental Training," *Science Advances* 3, no. 10 (October 4, 2017), https://doi.org/10.1126/sciadv.1700495.

Chapter 9

1. Bryan E. Robinson, Claudia Flowers, and Christopher Burris, "An Empirical Study of the Relationship between Self-Leadership and Workaholism 'Firefighter' Behaviors," *Journal of Self Leadership* 2 (2006): 91–98.

Chapter 10

1. Dotun Ogunyemi, Nathaniel I. Sugiyama, and Thomas M. Ferrari, "A Professional Development Workshop to Facilitate Self-Forgiveness," *Journal of Graduate Medical Education* 12, no. 3 (June 1, 2020): 335–39, https://doi.org/10.4300/jgme-d-19-00570.1.

Chapter 11

1. Sarah A. Myers et al., "Relationships between Self-Leadership, Psychological Symptoms, and Self-Related Thought in an Undergraduate Sample," *Psi Chi Journal of Psychological Research* 25, no. 2 (2020): 142–50, https://doi.org/10.24839/2325-7342.jn25.2.142; Michael Fitzgerald, "Cool, Calm, and Collected: The Associations between Self-Leadership and Adult Mental and Relational Health Outcomes," *The American Journal of Family Therapy* 50, no. 1 (February 2, 2021): 57–71, https://doi.org/10.1080/01926187.2020.1865218.

INDEX

D

E

F

R

S

ACKNOWLEDGMENTS

There are numerous beautiful souls who have contributed to bringing this book to fruition, starting with my husband, Zach. Your edits, clarity, and dedication to this project have infused every page with your Self energy. To my editor, Anne Barthel, thank you for your profound insights and commitment to these pages. To my IFS family, your support and shared love for the model have meant the world to me. A special thanks to my soul sister, Jessica Gibson, for loving and caring for every part of who I am.

ABOUT THE AUTHOR

Renowned spiritual teacher and #1 *New York Times* best-selling author **Gabby Bernstein** has been hailed as a "new thought leader" by Oprah Winfrey. Bernstein is the author of 10 books, including the bestsellers *The Universe Has Your Back*, *Super Attractor*, and *Happy Days*. Her empowering perspective and compassionate insights inspired *The New York Times* to call her "a role model for a new generation of spiritual seekers." In 2023 she launched the innovative gabby coaching membership to democratize spiritual self-help and be your coach—anytime, anywhere. In her weekly podcast, *Dear Gabby*, she connects with her community and offers insightful, real-time coaching, straight talk, and BIG LOVE. Through her presentations and generous Q&A sessions, Bernstein makes a major impact on individuals and organizations alike, and she has been sought after by groups such as Google, the AOL Build Series, TED Talks, Oprah's SuperSoul Sessions, and many more.

Bernstein frequently appears on *Today, Good Morning America*, and *Live with Kelly and Mark*, among other leading media outlets, to share her expertise in meditation, manifestation, and cultivating inner peace. She co-hosted the Guinness World Records' largest guided meditation with Deepak Chopra, and was named as one of Oprah's "SuperSoul 100"—a dynamic group of trailblazers whose vision and life's work are bringing a higher level of consciousness to the world. Bernstein is a highly sought-after keynote speaker, offering a profound message of peace that resonates with audiences of all kinds.

For more, visit **gabbybernstein.com**.

Hay House Titles of Related Interest

YOU CAN HEAL YOUR LIFE, the movie,
starring Louise Hay & Friends
(available as an online streaming video)
www.hayhouse.com/louise-movie

THE SHIFT, the movie,
starring Dr. Wayne W. Dyer
(available as an online streaming video)
www.hayhouse.com/the-shift-movie

***

HAPPY DAYS: The Guided Path from Trauma to Profound Freedom and Inner Peace

SUPER ATTRACTOR: Methods for Manifesting a Life beyond Your Wildest Dreams

THE UNIVERSE HAS YOUR BACK: From Fear to Faith

MIRACLES NOW: 108 Life-Changing Tools for Less Stress, More Flow, and Finding Your True Purpose

All of the above are available at your local bookstore,
or may be ordered by contacting Hay House (see next page).

***